THE
HOUSE OF COMMONS BOOK
OF
REMEMBRANCE
1914–1918

2nd Lieut. D. A. CARNEGIE.
Royal Field Artillery.

DAVID ALEXANDER CARNEGIE, second son of Lieut.-Col. the Hon. Douglas Carnegie, M.P. for Winchester, 1916-18, and grandson of the 9th Earl of Northesk, was born on January 15th, 1897. He was educated at Gresham's School, Holt, Norfolk, and instead of going to Cambridge, as was intended went to Woolwich. He received a commission in May, 1916, and was immediately sent out to France, where he took part in the engagements at Mametz and Contalmaison. He was killed in action by the explosion of an enemy shell in his battery at Brielen, near Ypres, on the 2nd of April, 1917, and was buried at Ferme-Oliver military cemetery at Elverdinghe in Flanders.

The Colonel commanding his Brigade wrote:—

> He was a splendidly gallant fellow who has done magnificent work always. He could always be absolutely depended upon, and his powers of observation and intuition were exceptional. His reports were always reliable.
>
> Both officers and men were most awfully fond of him.

THE HOUSE OF COMMONS BOOK OF REMEMBRANCE 1914-1918

Compiled and Edited by
EDWARD WHITAKER MOSS-BLUNDELL

The Naval & Military Press Ltd

Published by
The Naval & Military Press Ltd
5 Riverside, Brambleside, Bellbrook
Industrial Estate, Uckfield, East Sussex,
TN22 1QQ England

Tel: +44 (0) 1825 749494
Fax: +44 (0) 1825 765701

www.naval-military-press.com
www.nmarchive.com

*In reprinting in facsimile from the original, any imperfections are inevitably reproduced
and the quality may fall short of modern type and cartographic standards.*

TO THE
MEMBERS AND OFFICERS
OF BOTH HOUSES OF PARLIAMENT
AND THE
SONS OF MEMBERS AND OFFICERS
OF THE HOUSE OF COMMONS
WHO IN THE GREAT WAR
CONSUMMATED WITH THEIR LIVES THE
TRADITIONS OF PUBLIC SERVICE
IN THE CAUSE OF
RIGHT AND LIBERTY
THIS RECORD IS DEDICATED IN
HOMAGE AND AFFECTION

INTRODUCTION

THE record of the names of Members of Parliament, of their sons, and of the staff of the House of Commons who fell in the War demanded, and has received, special commemoration in the Memorial standing at the head of Westminster Hall.

This volume provides for us survivors, and for future generations, a fuller biography of those gallant men than that memorial can adequately supply; and it could find no more fitting home than in the lobby of the House, where their presence was familiar, their voices heard, their votes recorded and their work done.

The Members were of all political parties and creeds, but when the call of country came they forgot the one and set aside the other. Private interests, domestic ties, professional occupations, and legitimate ambitions vanished. None were for a Party and all were for the State.

They made their response to the sudden summons whole-heartedly and devotedly, a splendid example to their contemporaries and their descendants. As they had been the chosen spokesmen of the people in the Council Chamber, so they became the representatives of the nation in the Field. The same qualities which gained for them civic distinction in Parliament enabled them to lead and direct their subordinate comrades-in-arms and inspire confidence and achieve the popularity which was theirs in camp, in trenches and in battle.

"Of conspicuous men the whole world is the tomb, and it is not only inscriptions on tablets which chronicle their fame, but rather unwritten memorials living for ever not upon visible monuments but in the heart of mankind."

So we read in the funeral oration of Pericles, and so with our lost friends. Their memorial is inscribed in the hearts of their fellow Members and acquaintances:—

"Aere perennius."

The memory of the part they played in the great comradeship of the House of Commons and the greater comradeship of the battlefield will be with us while life lasts and, when we are no more, will be a precious relic and a noble incentive to the great call of duty.

ULLSWATER,
Speaker of the House of Commons
during the Great War, 1914-1918.

CONTENTS

	PAGE
INTRODUCTION	vii

SECTION I:
PEERS OF PARLIAMENT 3
OFFICERS OF THE HOUSE OF LORDS 4

SECTION II: MEMBERS
OF THE
HOUSE OF COMMONS 7–47

CAPTAIN THE HON. T. C. R. AGAR-ROBARTES	7
LIEUT.-COL. THE HON. G. V. BARING	9
MAJOR F. BENNETT-GOLDNEY	11
LIEUT.-COL. D. F. CAMPBELL, D.S.O.	13
CAPTAIN H. T. CAWLEY	15
CAPTAIN THE HON. O. CAWLEY	17
LIEUT.-COL. P. A. CLIVE	19
LIEUT.-COL. LORD N. E. CRICHTON-STUART	21
CAPTAIN J. J. ESMONDE	23
MAJOR V. FLEMING, D.S.O.	25
LIEUT. W. G. C. GLADSTONE	27
MAJOR P. K. GLAZEBROOK, D.S.O.	28
LIEUT. T. M. KETTLE	30
MAJOR THE HON. C. H. LYELL	32
LIEUT. THE HON. F. W. S. MCLAREN	34
LIEUT. THE HON. C. T. MILLS	36
CAPTAIN THE HON. A. E. B. O'NEILL	38
CAPTAIN THE RT. HON. N. J. A. PRIMROSE, P.C., M.C.	40
LIEUT. THE VISCOUNT QUENINGTON	42
MAJOR W. H. K. REDMOND	43
LIEUT.-COL. LORD A. G. B. THYNNE, D.S.O.	45
LIEUT. THE HON. W. L. C. WALROND	47

SECTION III: OFFICERS
OF THE
HOUSE OF COMMONS   PAGE 51–61

LIEUT. R. N. M. BAILEY	51
2ND LIEUT. R. W. T. COX	53
LIEUT. V. W. D. FOX	54
MAJOR H. S. GREEN	55
CORPORAL R. LANCHBERY	57
2ND LIEUT. W. K. SANDERSON	58
LIEUT. F. SEYMOUR	60

SECTION IV: SONS
OF
MEMBERS
OF THE
HOUSE OF COMMONS   65–170

LANCE-CORPORAL J. C. ADAMSON	65
LIEUT. J. S. AINSWORTH	67
LIEUT.-COL. D. K. ANDERSON, M.C.	68
LIEUT. C. K. ANDERSON	69
CAPTAIN THE HON. ARTHUR ANNESLEY	70
LIEUT. D. M. ARCHDALE	71
LIEUT. RAYMOND ASQUITH	72
2ND LIEUT. A. S. BALFOUR	74
CAPTAIN C. W. BANBURY	75
2ND LIEUT. H. BARNES	77
CAPTAIN R. N. BARRAN	78
2ND LIEUT. E. A. BEAUCHAMP	79
2ND LIEUT. F. H. BETHELL	81
2ND LIEUT. H. F. BOLES	82
LIEUT. H. J. BOYTON	84
SUB-LIEUT. W. P. BRACE	85
2ND LIEUT. G. C. BRASSEY	86
2ND LIEUT. A. H. ROSDEW BURN	87
LIEUT.-COMMANDER P. S. CAMPBELL	89
2ND LIEUT. F. L. CAREW	90
MAJOR E. H. H. CARLILE	91
2ND LIEUT. D. A. CARNEGIE	92
MAJOR J. S. CAWLEY	93
CAPTAIN R. G. H. CHALONER	95
2ND LIEUT. A. J. F. CHAMBERS	96
CAPTAIN T. V. BARTLEY DENNISS	97

	PAGE
2ND LIEUT. G. J. ESMONDE	98
MIDSHIPMAN J. H. GRATTAN ESMONDE	99
CAPTAIN J. E. FIENNES	100
MAJOR THE REV. J. J. FITZGIBBON, S.J., M.C.	101
CAPTAIN M. J. FITZGIBBON	103
CAPTAIN M. A. FITZROY	105
2ND LIEUT. J. FORSTER	106
LIEUT. A. H. FORSTER	108
CAPTAIN W. HARMOOD-BANNER	109
CAPTAIN D. HENDERSON	110
LIEUT. C. C. HENRY	111
CAPTAIN G. G. HERMON-HODGE	112
2ND LIEUT J. P. HERMON-HODGE	113
2ND LIEUT. G. M. HEWART	114
CAPTAIN C. G. R. HIBBERT	115
LIEUT. W. P. HINDS	116
2ND LIEUT. I. G. JOHN	117
CAPTAIN J. K. LAW	119
LIEUT. C. J. LAW	121
LIEUT. H. LOGAN	122
BRIGADIER-GENERAL W. LONG, C.M.G., D.S.O.	123
LIEUT. G. A. LOYD	125
LIEUT. D. C. D. MACMASTER	126
2ND LIEUT. G. T. G. MCMICKING	127
CAPTAIN G. C. N. NICHOLSON	128
LIEUT. W. H. E. NIELD	129
LIEUT. H. N. NUTTALL	131
2ND LIEUT. W. J. O'MALLEY	132
LIEUT. W. P. ORDE-POWLETT	133
2ND LIEUT. G. V. PEARCE	134
LIEUT. R. H. PIKE PEASE	135
LIEUT. T. W. POLLARD	137
CAPTAIN C. T. A. POLLOCK	138
LIEUT. R. J. PROTHERO	140
SUB-LIEUT. J. F. ROYDS	141
2ND LIEUT. T. W. RUSSELL	142
2ND LIEUT. J. H. CLAVELL SALTER	143
CAPTAIN A. P. I. SAMUELS	144
CAPTAIN C. G. SEELY	145
LIEUT. F. R. SEELY	147
2ND LIEUT. D. J. SHEEHAN	148
2ND LIEUT. M. J. SHEEHAN	150
LIEUT. W. E. D. SHORTT	151
LIEUT. J. F. SMALLWOOD, M.C.	153
CAPTAIN E. B. SMALLWOOD, M.C.	154
MAJOR G. H. SOAMES	155

	PAGE
Major M. G. Soames	156
Lieut. C. Stanton	157
Lieut. V. A. Strauss	158
2nd Lieut. H. Tennant	159
Lieut. J. P. Thorne	160
Private W. E. Thorne	161
Lieut. E. S. Turton	162
Private B. Wadsworth	164
Captain A. Walsh, M.C.	165
Lieut. C. J. Warner	166
2nd Lieut. T. H. B. Webb	167
Private J. N. Williams	168
Lieut. W. Young	169
Lieut. C. F. Younger	170

Section V: SONS OF OFFICERS OF THE HOUSE OF COMMONS 173–181

Lieut. A. R. Garton	173
Lieut. R. W. Garton	174
2nd Lieut. E. W. J. Johnson	175
2nd Lieut. B. Moon	176
Lieut. W. D. Nicholson	178
Lieut. A. S. Nicholson	179
2nd Lieut. G. Norman	180
Sergeant P. J. Turtle	181

Section VI: APPENDIX 183–196

Note :—The lists contained in the Appendix give the place and exact site of the graves of the officers and men who fell. Where no grave exists, the War Memorial on which the name is commemorated is also given.

I.

PEERS OF PARLIAMENT

OFFICERS
OF THE
HOUSE OF LORDS

PEERS OF PARLIAMENT

SHELLEY LEOPOLD LAURENCE, 5th Baron ABINGER
WYNDHAM WENTWORTH, 3rd Baron BRABOURNE
HENRY BLIGH FORTESCUE, 5th Baron CONGLETON
VICTOR GEORGE HENRY FRANCIS, 5th Marquess CONYNGHAM.
ARTHUR REGINALD, 5th Baron De FREYNE
GILBERT GEORGE REGINALD, 8th Earl De La WARR
CHARLES WILLIAM REGINALD, 2nd Earl of FEVERSHAM
HENRY GORELL, 2nd Baron GORELL, D.S.O.
THOMAS CAREW, 3rd Baron KESTEVEN
HORATIO HERBERT, 1st Earl KITCHENER OF KHARTOUM, K.G., K.P., G.C.B., O.M., G.C.S.I., G.C.M.G., G.C.I.E.
JOHN MACLEAN, 2nd Baron LLANGATTOCK
THOMAS, 5th EARL OF LONGFORD and BARON SILCHESTER, K.P., M.V.O.
AUBERON THOMAS, 8th Baron LUCAS and 11th Baron DINGWALL
LIONEL GEORGE CARROLL, 16th Baron PETRE
WILLIAM JOHN LYDSTON, 7th Earl POULETT
FREDERICK SLEIGH, 1st Earl ROBERTS, V.C., K.G., K.P., G.C.B., O.M., G.C.S.I., G.C.I.E.
WILLIAM EDWARD, 5th Earl of ROSSE
JAMES, 11th Earl of SEAFIELD and 3rd Baron STRATHSPEY
HENRY MOLYNEUX PAGET, 19th Earl of SUFFOLK and 12th Earl of BERKSHIRE
GEORGE FRANCIS AUGUSTUS, 8th Baron VERNON

OFFICERS OF THE HOUSE OF LORDS

CAPTAIN ROBERT AMBREY COURT, 8th Yorks (West Riding) Regiment.
LIEUTENANT WILLIAM GEORGE GRESHAM LEVESON-GOWER, Coldstream Guards.

Peers of Parliament and Officers of the House of Lords who fell in the War are commemorated in the Royal Gallery, where the House of Lords War Memorial is placed.

II.

MEMBERS
OF THE
HOUSE OF COMMONS

CAPTAIN THE HON. T. C. R. AGAR-ROBARTES

Coldstream Guards

THOMAS CHARLES REGINALD AGAR-ROBARTES was the oldest son of the 6th Viscount Clifden. He was born on May 22nd, 1880, and went to Miss Evans' House at Eton in the Lent Half, 1894, leaving in July, 1899, as a member of Pop and with his House Colours.

After three years at Christ Church, Oxford, where he was president of Bullingdon, Master of the Drag, and played Polo for Oxford against Cambridge in 1903, he entered Parliament as Member for the St. Austell Division of Cornwall in 1908, having been returned previously for Bodmin, in 1906, but unseated on petition.

Vitality and independence were the keynotes of his character. He threw himself into the task of the moment with his full energy and with a zest and enjoyment of life which nothing could damp. Indifferent to criticism and quite undaunted by opposition, he pursued his own course, living every hour of his life to the full. Such a man makes himself felt in every situation, and he was always a force to be reckoned with and by no means to be discounted whether at school or at the university, in politics and in the world of sport. An air of casualness hid a quick mind and a shrewd judgment, and it was no surprise to his friends that his name was coming rapidly to the fore in the House. His attitude in the Irish controversy was typical alike of his courageous independence and of his capacity for reaching a practical and definite decision.

He was exactly the type of man required when the storm broke in August, 1914. All the essential qualities of the soldier were there—complete fearlessness, grit, rapid decision—leadership.

On the outbreak of War he joined the Royal Bucks Hussars, but finding himself still in England in January, 1915, and determined at all costs to get to the Front, he obtained a transfer into the Coldstream Guards as Lieutenant, went out to France in February, and was promoted Captain in June. He was wounded near Loos on September 28th while superintending the rescue of wounded men, and died on September 30th. About half an hour before he was fatally wounded he left his trench in broad daylight in the face of heavy machine gun fire, and with an N.C.O. succeeded in bringing in a severely wounded sergeant.

He was buried in Lapugnoy Military Cemetery, near Béthune.

One of his brother officers wrote as follows:

"His company attacked on the night of the 27th and captured a position which we afterwards managed to hold. During this attack he walked about absolutely fearlessly and never could be persuaded to take cover of any sort. He behaved splendidly, and showed his men such an excellent example that they achieved a thing which would otherwise have been impossible. Ever since he has been out here he has shown himself absolutely fearless, and his bravery was wonderful. The few remaining of his company are in despair at losing him. They worshipped the ground he trod on."

Captain Agar-Robartes was mentioned in despatches, and recommended for the award of the Victoria Cross for conspicuous gallantry in the field on September 28th, 1915.

LIEUT.-COL. THE HON. G. V. BARING

Coldstream Guards

GUY VICTOR BARING, fourth son of the 4th Lord Ashburton, was born on February 26th, 1873. Educated at Eton and Sandhurst, he joined the Coldstream Guards in 1893, and served with the regiment in the South African War, 1899-1900. He was present at the battles of Belmont, Graspan, Modder River, Magersfontein, and Driefontein, and at the occupation of Bloemfontein. He was also in the advance to Pretoria. He was mentioned in despatches, and received the Queen's Medal with three clasps. In command of a detachment of the Coldstream Guards, he went in 1900 with the Australia and New Zealand Imperial Representative Corps to be present at the inauguration of Lord Hopetoun as first Governor-General of the Commonwealth of Australia. After this, he was attached to the King's African Rifles and served as a special service officer in the Jubuland Expedition, 1901, against the Ogaden Somalis, for which he received a medal with clasp. He left the Coldstream Guards in 1913.

He was a keen sportsman and had travelled extensively in search of sport in the United States, Canada, Australia, New Zealand, Somaliland and the British East Africa Protectorate. Colonel Baring had the unusual experience of being a successful Candidate in three General Elections in five years; he was first elected Member for Winchester in January, 1906, and was again elected with increased majorities in January and December, 1910. As a speaker, he always commanded attention, imparting into his speeches something of his own attractive personality.

On the outbreak of War in August, 1914, he rejoined the Coldstream Guards, remaining at Windsor in command of a training company. He went out to France in July, 1915, as Second in Command of the 4th (Pioneer) Battalion. After the Battle of Loos, he was given command of the 1st Battalion.

In the early morning of September 15th, 1916, in the course of the operations on the Somme, the 1st and 2nd Guards Brigades moved forward to the attack along the Ginchy-Lesbœufs road. For the first time in the history of the regiment three battalions of Coldstream Guards attacked in line together, advancing, as one eye-witness described the scene, "as steadily as though they were walking down the Mall." The 1st Battalion went into action with 17 officers and 690 other ranks; they came out of the battle with 3 officers, one of whom was wounded, and 221 other ranks.

Colonel Baring, who fell in this action, had proved himself a capable commander and his death was deeply regretted by all ranks.

He was buried in The Citadel New Military Cemetery, near Fricourt.

Colonel Baring was twice mentioned in despatches.

MAJOR F. BENNETT-GOLDNEY

Royal Army Service Corps

FRANCIS BENNETT-GOLDNEY, born in 1865, was the second son of Dr. Sebastian Evans, LL.D., author, artist and journalist, his mother—whose maiden name he assumed in 1892—being the youngest daughter of Francis Bennett-Goldney, one of the founders of the London Joint Stock Bank.

Educated privately, he was a Fellow of the Society of Antiquaries and member of several Archæological and Scientific Societies; connoisseur of works of art, notably Anglo-Saxon antiquities and early English pottery, and joint author with his father of various historical and other works.

From 1905 to 1911 he was Mayor of Canterbury, and his benefactions to the city were considerable. During part of his mayoralty Mr. Bennett-Goldney was freely criticized because of a series of very vigorous speeches on the subject of the German peril, but he never wavered in his convictions, which were based on his observations on the Continent, where he had travelled extensively.

He was elected Member for Canterbury in December, 1910, and early in 1916 attracted attention by a vigorous criticism of the administration of the Air Service.

In the early days of the War, when refugees and the wounded were coming over in large numbers from across the Channel, he did good work in helping to find accommodation for them, and for this service received the thanks of the Army Council. After a period of special recruiting duty in Yorkshire and Durham for the Royal Engineers' Tunnelling Companies, he was gazetted Honorary Assistant Military Attaché in Paris early in 1918. He died on July 27th, 1918, in an American Hospital at Brest from injuries sustained some time previously in a motor-car accident, and was buried at St. Germain-en-Laye, near Paris.

He formerly held a Captain's commission in the 6th Middlesex Regiment (Militia).

LIEUT.-COL. D. F. CAMPBELL, D.S.O.

Duke of Wellington's (West Riding) Regiment

DUNCAN FREDERICK CAMPBELL was a Canadian by birth, his family, which was of Argyllshire origin, having left Inverary for Canada in 1799. He was born at Toronto on April 24th, 1876, and educated at Trinity School, Port Hope, and Trinity University, Toronto, where he graduated with honours in mental and moral philosophy. His grandfather was first Member of Parliament for Toronto; his uncle, Sir Thomas Galt, Chief Justice of Ontario, and a cousin, Sir James Edgar, was formerly Speaker of the House of Commons, Ottawa. He joined the Lancashire Fusiliers in 1898, and served in various parts of the world, including Malta, Egypt, Gibraltar, the West Indies and South Africa. In the South African War he was several times mentioned in despatches by Lord Roberts and Sir Redvers Buller, and gained the D.S.O. In 1908 he transferred to the Black Watch.

Colonel Campbell retired from the Army in order to take up a political career. He contested Mid-Lanark in 1906, Paisley in 1910 (January), and North Ayrshire, unsuccessfully, in December, 1910, but he succeeded in winning the seat in December, 1911, at a by-election caused by the appointment of the sitting member to be Solicitor-General for Scotland. Soon after the outbreak of the European War, Colonel Campbell was transferred to the Gordon Highlanders, and was severely wounded at Ypres in November, 1914, while leading his men in an attack on an enemy trench. Notwithstanding this, he continued fighting and succeeded with his men in taking the trench, but was again struck by a shell. After being in hospital in Paris, he came home on furlough. On regaining the use of his arm, he was promoted to the rank of Colonel, and put in command of a battalion of the West Riding Regiment. He died at Southwold, Suffolk, on the 4th September, 1916, and was buried in Kilmarnock Cemetery, Ayrshire.

Colonel Campbell was twice mentioned in despatches.

CAPTAIN H. T. CAWLEY

6th Battalion The Manchester Regiment, T.F.

HAROLD THOMAS CAWLEY, second son of Sir Frederick Cawley, Bart., M.P. for Prestwich Division, S.E. Lancashire, was born on June 12th, 1878.

He entered Rugby School in 1891, and went up to New College, Oxford, in 1895, where he took a Second Class in the History School. He was called to the Bar by the Inner Temple in 1902, and practised on the Northern Circuit. He was elected Member of Parliament for the Heywood Division of South-East Lancashire in January, 1910, and held the seat up to the time of his death. He was Parliamentary Secretary, unpaid, to the President of the Board of Education, the Right Honourable W. Runciman, in 1910–11, and to the Home Secretary, the Right Honourable Reginald McKenna, from December, 1911, onwards. He was a good all-round sportsman and a first-rate man to hounds. He won several Point-to-Point Races, including the "Bar Point-to-Point" in 1914.

For twelve years he had been an Officer in the 6th Manchesters, and as an old Territorial Officer he volunteered for active service on the outbreak of War. He went to Egypt as Aide-de-Camp to Major-General W. Douglas in August, 1914, and to the Dardanelles in May, 1915.

Many of the Officers of his Battalion were killed in the assault on the Turkish trenches at Krithia on June

4th and 5th, and it was his constant wish to exchange the comparative safety of Divisional Headquarters for work with his own men. He accordingly returned to his Battalion early in September, and fell in action a fortnight later, September 24th, 1915. He was buried in the Lancashire Landing Cemetery, Helles, Gallipoli.

A Manchester Territorial, in an interesting letter home, relates an incident illustrating Captain Cawley's bravery, which took place before he returned to his Battalion:

"Captain Cawley was a very brave and unassuming gentleman; one of his exploits is worth recounting. A small ammunition cart had been taken up the principal nullah, where the men proceeded to unload in order to carry the cases to the dug-out. The enemy spotted this waggon and immediately started to shell it vigorously with shrapnel. Naturally there was a slight hesitancy on the part of the men unloading as to what was the wisest thing to do. Captain Cawley settled the situation by getting off his horse into the cart and handing the boxes down in double-quick time. After the vehicle was clear he coolly rode away."

CAPTAIN THE HON. O. CAWLEY

Shropshire Yeomanry and 10th (Shropshire and Cheshire Yeomanry) Battalion The King's (Shropshire Light Infantry), T.F.

OSWALD CAWLEY, fourth and youngest son of Lord Cawley of Prestwich, formerly Sir Frederick Cawley, Bart., M.P. for Prestwich, was born on October 7th, 1882.

He entered Rugby School in 1896 and left in 1900. He was elected an Exhibitioner of New College, Oxford, and, after training on the Continent, went up to New College and took his degree with Second Class honours in History. On going down from Oxford he joined his father's business, becoming Assistant Manager of the Heaton Mills Bleaching Company. In 1911 he went round the world, staying some time in Japan and India. He spent most of his leisure in philanthropic work, being particularly interested in Lads' Clubs and the Boy Scouts movement.

He joined the Shropshire Yeomanry in May, 1914, and went out to Egypt in January, 1916. His Regiment was subsequently converted into the 10th Battalion The King's (Shropshire Light Infantry), and he served with it in Palestine. He took part in the second Battle of Gaza and other engagements in that country.

In January, 1918, when his father was raised to the peerage, he was invited to contest the Prestwich Division of Lancashire and was elected by a large majority, after stipulating that he should not be expected to remain in England during the War.

In April, 1918, he accompanied his Battalion to France, and, shortly after being promoted Captain, fell while leading his Company in a charge, after having been twice wounded, near Merville, on August 22nd, 1918. He was buried in Néry Communal Cemetery.

LIEUT.-COLONEL P. A. CLIVE

Grenadier Guards

PERCY ARCHER CLIVE was the eldest son of Charles Meysey Bolton Clive, Esquire, J.P., of Whitfield Court, Herefordshire, and Lady Katherine Feilding, youngest daughter of the 7th Earl of Denbigh. He was born in 1873, educated at Eton and Sandhurst and entered the Grenadier Guards in 1891, being appointed Captain in 1899 and retiring in 1901. He served in West Africa in 1898, in the Expedition to Annan, and in South Africa in 1899-1901 when he received the Queen's Medal with five clasps. Whilst fighting in South Africa he was elected M.P. for South Herefordshire. He acted as Parliamentary private secretary (unpaid) to Mr. Austen Chamberlain.

Col. Clive served actively with the forces from the beginning of the War, rejoining the colours on August 5th, 1914. In the following November he returned to his own regiment, the 1st Battalion of the Grenadier Guards. He was with the Battalion through much heavy fighting in France in the first winter of the War and in the following April was awarded the Legion of Honour by the French Government for a daring exploit in the trenches. Accompanied by Major Foulkes, Col. (then Capt.) Clive ventured beyond the British lines in the dark and made a successful reconnaissance. They explored a section of the German trenches which proved to be empty, and then came upon a group of the enemy in a connecting trench. They were surrounded by Germans but managed to escape unhurt amid a shower of bullets, and having gained the valuable knowledge they had sought. The Legion of Honour was afterwards presented to Col. Clive by General Joffre and he was mentioned in one of Sir John French's despatches of the same month.

In August, 1915, Col. Clive was wounded in the head at Givenchy and invalided home. The following May he took command of the 7th Battalion East Yorkshire Regiment in France, being promoted Lieut.-Colonel. Not long afterwards he was again seriously wounded at Le Transloy sustaining a fractured thigh and a wound in the shoulder. On his recovery he was ordered for duty with the Southern Army at Brentwood, Essex, but later returned to France and was mentioned in Sir Douglas Haig's despatch of November 7th, 1917. He was killed in action at Bucquoy, in France, on April 5th, 1918, while helping a wounded officer, and was at that time attached to the 1/5th Lancashire Fusiliers. His body was not recovered, but his name is perpetuated on the Arras Memorial.

Colonel Clive was awarded the Legion of Honour, and the Croix de Guerre, and was twice mentioned in despatches.

LIEUT.-COL. LORD N. E. CRICHTON-STUART

6th Battn. Welch Regiment, T.F.

NINIAN EDWARD CRICHTON-STUART, second son of the 3rd Marquess of Bute, was born on May 15th, 1883.

He was educated at Harrow, and pursued his studies with much success, particularly in mathematics and languages. At that time it was intended that he should enter the Diplomatic Service. With this object in view he proceeded to Russia to continue his linguistic studies, but, being taken ill there, he came home to recuperate. After his recovery he went to Christ Church, Oxford, and while at the University made himself extremely popular, for Lord Ninian was a great sportsman, being a believer in sport as one of the backbones of our national life. He was a good shot, keen fisherman and very fond of motoring.

On leaving Oxford, after a successful career, he accepted a commission in 1903 in the 3rd Battalion (Militia) of the Queen's Own Cameron Highlanders. Subsequently he served for two years as an officer in the 1st Battalion, Scots Guards, leaving the regiment after his marriage in order to look after his estates in Scotland and to take up politics.

In December, 1910, he was elected Member for the United Boroughs of Cardiff, Cowbridge and Llantrisant; his memorable success at the second attempt thrilled the electors of Cardiff, and jubilant scenes followed the declaration of the poll.

As a Member of the House of Commons, Lord Ninian impressed all by his industry and conscientiousness. He was always accessible to his constituents, and constantly interested himself in questions of importance to Cardiff and its business affairs. He did much towards making the enfranchisement of leaseholds a matter of practical concern, and he was a frequent speaker against the disestablishment and disendowment of the Church in Wales.

On the outbreak of War, he took command of the 6th Welch Regiment at Glamorgan ports, protecting dock property, and so well was this duty performed and so high was the military efficiency to which the battalion had been raised that in October, 1914, Lord Ninian and his officers and men sailed for France—among the earliest Territorial battalions to land in the theatre of war.

In July, 1915, the regiment was transferred from the line of communications to the fighting lines, and there, as in the greyer, less exciting atmosphere behind the trenches, Lord Ninian preserved the same high qualities of heart and mind which had long since made him the idol of his men.

He fell in action at the Battle of Loos on October 2nd, 1915.

His regiment, his friends, and the wide constituency which he served, united in paying homage to a brave officer and a gallant gentleman.

He was buried in Béthune Town Cemetery.

CAPTAIN J. J. ESMONDE

Royal Army Medical Corps

JOHN JOSEPH ESMONDE, second son of James Esmonde, Esquire, D.L., J.P., of Drominagh, Borrisokane, Co. Tipperary, Ireland, was born on January 27th, 1862, and was educated at Clongowes Wood College, Co. Kildare, and at Stonyhurst and Oscott. A cousin of Sir Thomas Esmonde, he was a member of a distinguished Irish family which has played a large part in Irish history. He studied medicine in Dublin, and, after a short appointment at the Curragh, practised in England for twenty-four years. In 1909 he returned to Ireland, taking up his residence at Drominagh, his country place on the Shannon, and later threw himself earnestly into the Irish National Volunteer movement, becoming honorary Colonel of the Nenagh Regiment of the Volunteers. As an agriculturist, he was largely interested in a scheme for the manufacture of synthetic rubber from artichokes.

He was returned unopposed to Parliament in 1910 as Nationalist Member for North Tipperary, and retained his seat until his death. One of the most familiar and cheery figures in the Members' lobby, Dr. Esmonde was a strange mixture of Nationalism and that Conservatism which always underlies the Irish character, and he brought those qualities into daily play in the House.

On the outbreak of War he took a leading part in urging that Nationalist Ireland should take her part in frustrating the designs of the common enemy. He was appointed to a temporary commission as Captain in the Royal Army Medical Corps in January, 1915, and served at Tipperary Barracks until his death at Drominagh on April 17th, 1915, from pneumonia and heart failure consequent on the strain of overwork.

He was buried in Terryglass R.C. Churchyard, Co. Tipperary.

Captain Esmonde's two elder sons obtained commissions and served in France; his second son fell in action and is commemorated elsewhere in this volume.

MAJOR VALENTINE FLEMING, D.S.O.

Queen's Own Oxfordshire Hussars

VALENTINE FLEMING was the son of Robert Fleming, Esquire, of Joyce Grove, Nettlebed. He was born on February 17th, 1882, and was educated at Eton where he was in the Eight in 1900. On leaving school he matriculated at Magdalen College, Oxford, and rowed in his College eight, which won the Ladies' Plate, and the four that won the Visitors' Plate, at Henley.

He took his degree with Second Class honours in History and was called to the Bar in 1907, after leaving Oxford, becoming subsequently a member of the firm of Robert Fleming & Company, merchant bankers. He was a very keen and expert deer stalker and he also owned and hunted a pack of basset hounds.

Before long he determined to enter public life and was elected Member of Parliament for the Henley Division of Oxfordshire in 1910. Though an energetic member of the House, he found time to learn his work thoroughly as a yeomanry officer and went through most of the courses of instruction open to officers. He was in consequence a capable soldier when the War broke out and was soon sent to the front. After nearly three years of incessant fighting he fell on May 20th, 1917, at Guillemont Farm, near Épéhy, where with seventy men he had held an advanced post to which the Germans attached much importance. The seventy beat off an attack of two hundred of the enemy, but not before he himself fell.

The regiment lost in him not only a brave and capable officer but also a character of singular charm and attraction. Those who knew him best perhaps remember chiefly the laughter and talk full of shrewd thrusts which enlivened good days and bad, merry evenings in billets, wet and anxious nights in trenches. He left a gap that could not be filled, a memory that could not be forgotten. He was buried in Ste. Emilie British Cemetery, Villers-Faucon.

Major Fleming was awarded the D.S.O., and was twice mentioned in despatches.

LIEUT. W. G. C. GLADSTONE

Royal Welch Fusiliers

WILLIAM GLYNNE CHARLES GLADSTONE, born July 14th, 1885, was the only son of William Henry Gladstone, Esquire, and grandson of the Rt. Hon. W. E. Gladstone (Prime Minister 1869, 1880-5-6, and 1892-4). He was educated at Eton and New College, Oxford, and was President of the Oxford Union in 1907. He was for a time Honorary Attaché to the British Embassy at Washington.

Mr. Gladstone was returned for the Kilmarnock Burghs in 1911, and during his four years' Membership of the House of Commons had won for himself universal regard and esteem. On his return from Washington he was appointed Lord-Lieutenant of Flintshire and discharged the duties of the post with zeal and earnestness, and when War broke out was active in promoting recruiting. Later, he decided that it was his duty to offer himself for military service; he applied for and received a commission as second lieutenant in the Welch Fusiliers on Sept. 21st, 1914. He left for France with his regiment on March 15th, and after three weeks' service at the front was killed in the trenches near Laventie on April 13th, 1915.

He was buried in Hawarden Churchyard, Flintshire.

Mr. Gladstone was the second Member of the House of Commons to fall in the service of his country.

MAJOR P. K. GLAZEBROOK, D.S.O.

King's Shropshire Light Infantry

PHILIP KIRKLAND GLAZEBROOK was the only son of T. K. Glazebrook, Esquire, of Twemlow Hall, Holmes Chapel, Cheshire, and was born on December 24th, 1880. He was educated at Eton and New College, Oxford, and entered Parliament as Member for Manchester South, in 1912, when, after a spirited fight over the National Insurance Bill, the Government Candidate was defeated by 579 votes. He had been in the Cheshire Yeomanry for many years before the War, and when the Yeomanry were dismounted the Cheshires were then attached to the King's Shropshire Light Infantry. Major Glazebrook sailed for Egypt in March, 1916, and served in Palestine. In action at Et Tireh in the third Battle of Gaza, on November 29th, 1917, he behaved with great gallantry, seized and occupied the hill Sheikh Hassan and held the village of Et Tireh until a strong counter-attack of the Turks, with heavy shell fire, to which our guns made no reply, rendered the position untenable. Under orders to retire, Major Glazebrook succeeded with great skill in extricating his small force and bringing in all his wounded. A few months later, he was present at the occupation of Kurunthal and Jericho by the British troops; on the resumption of the advance Northwards to Wadi Stour the battalion came again under shell fire and he fell on March 7th,

1918, at Bireh, near Jerusalem. He was buried in the Jerusalem War Cemetery.

Major Glazebrook, who had just been awarded the D.S.O. for his fine handling of the situation at Et Tireh a few months previously, was a great loss to his battalion, being an officer who inspired all ranks with the greatest confidence.

LIEUT. T. M. KETTLE

Royal Dublin Fusiliers

THOMAS MICHAEL KETTLE, third son of Andrew J. Kettle, Esquire, was born on February 9th, 1880. He was educated at Clongowes Wood College, Co. Kildare, proceeding in 1897 to University College, Dublin, where he graduated in mental and moral science and won the Gold Medal for Oratory. After a year spent on the Continent, he entered the King's Inns as a Law Student in 1902; in 1905 he won the Victoria Prize and was called to the Irish Bar in 1906. He entered Parliament at a by-election in July, 1906, as Member for East Tyrone, with a majority of only 19, but was again returned at the General Election in January, 1910. In 1908 he went to America as envoy on a Home Rule Mission, and having been appointed Professor of Economics in the National University of Ireland in 1909, he did not further contest East Tyrone at the ensuing General Election in December, 1910.

At one time editor of the "Nationalist," he wrote, translated and edited several works and pamphlets of a miscellaneous character.

In 1912 he was one of the prominent Irishmen identified with the foundation of the National Volunteers, and when War broke out was engaged in Belgium buying rifles for them. In August and September, 1914, he acted as War Correspondent of the *Daily News* in Belgium, and in November of that year obtained a commission in the 7th Battalion Leinster Regiment. His oratorical gifts and prestige as a Nationalist were an asset to the Recruiting Committee; he was employed on this work until July, 1916, when, after protests at being kept at home, he was sent to France with the Royal Dublin Fusiliers.

He behaved with distinction at Guillemont, and, later, as acting Captain, fell in action while leading his men with great gallantry, at Ginchy, in the Battle of the Somme, on September 9th, 1916.

His body was not recovered, but his name is perpetuated on the Thiepval Memorial.

A brother officer wrote of him:

"It was with reluctance that he discarded the professor's gown for the soldier's uniform; but once the choice was made he threw himself into his new profession because he believed he was serving Ireland and humanity by so doing. When he fell in the hottest corner of the fighting at Ginchy, he was leading his men with a gallantry and judgment that would almost certainly have won him official recognition had he lived. He was one of the finest officers we had with us. The men worshipped him, and would have followed him to the ends of the earth."

MAJOR THE HON. C. H. LYELL

Royal Garrison Artillery

CHARLES HENRY LYELL was the only son of the 1st Baron Lyell of Kinnordy. Born in 1875, he was educated at Eton and New College, Oxford. In 1906 he was appointed Parliamentary Private Secretary to Sir Edward Grey, and in February, 1911, to Mr. Asquith. He represented East Dorset from March, 1904, to January, 1910, when he unsuccessfully contested West Edinburgh, and he sat as member for South Edinburgh from April, 1910, to May, 1917. He was gazetted captain in the Fife Royal Garrison Artillery in September, 1914, and obtained his majority in May, 1915. He was on active service until 1917 when he was badly burnt by an explosion of cordite and remained in hospital in Devonshire for some time. He resigned his seat in Parliament and later in 1917 returned to the front; he was in command of a battery at Ypres when he was ordered to Washington as Assistant Military Attaché, and died there on October 18th, 1918, of heart failure following influenza. He was buried in Arlington National Cemetery, Fort Myer, Virginia, U.S.A.

General McLachlan wrote of him:

"He had endeared himself to everyone whom he met in this Country, particularly in Washington where he was universally beloved. His memory will long remain in the hearts of the people out here; for I think I can confidently say that no British Officer ever succeeded in so short a time in so completely winning his way into the affections of the people of this Country. For my own part I mourn the loss of a dear friend and a wise counsellor."

Major Lyell was mentioned in despatches.

LIEUT. THE HON. F. W. S. McLAREN

Royal Flying Corps

FRANCIS WALTER STAFFORD McLAREN, second son of Lord Aberconway of Bodnant, was born on June 6th, 1886. He was educated at Eton, where he did well both in work and games, and got his house colours at football, proceeding to Balliol College, Oxford, at the age of 19. Here he was amongst that brilliant little group of Balliol men whose early promise was cut short by the War. He took an Honours Degree in History, was an ardent member of the Union and took a prominent part in political discussions as a champion of Free Trade. In 1910 he was elected Member for the Spalding Division of Lincolnshire, and was the youngest member of that Parliament. He became Parliamentary Private Secretary to the Rt. Hon. L. Harcourt, then First Commissioner of Works and later Secretary of State for the Colonies. He had considerable success as Seconder of the Address on the Opening of Parliament in February, 1913, when by a rare coincidence, his father was moving the Address in the House of Lords on the same occasion.

On the outbreak of the War he joined the R.N.V.R. and was sent to Gallipoli with the armoured cars. On one occasion, when his car was disabled and the driver wounded, he carried the man back to the dressing-station and next day with another officer recovered the car. Owing to an attack of dysentery he was sent to Egypt, but, seeing little chance of active service there, decided to come home and join the Royal Flying Corps. While undergoing a course in Scotland he met with an accident at Montrose, on the final flight of his training, on August 30th, 1917, and his machine dived into the sea. When he was picked up three minutes later by a fishing boat it was found that he had fractured his skull in the fall. He was buried in Busbridge Churchyard, Surrey.

As a boy he always showed great care to understand, and give due consideration in any discussion to, the point of view and the arguments of an opponent. This characteristic remained his and explains why he made many friends among political opponents, and no enemies.

Speaking of him in the House of Commons on October 29th, 1917, Mr. Asquith said: "We have lost one of the youngest and most loved of our members, Francis McLaren, cut off in a youth of radiant promise, still untarnished by disappointment, with clear and firm conviction, a faithful and loyal friend, and those who knew him best knew how much there was in the coming years to be hoped for."

LIEUT. THE HON. C. T. MILLS

2nd Battalion Scots Guards

CHARLES THOMAS MILLS, eldest son of the 2nd Lord Hillingdon, was born on March 13th, 1887. He was educated at Eton and Magdalen College, Oxford, and played golf for Oxford against Cambridge in 1907 and 1908. He took his degree in 1908, and at the General Election of January, 1910, was elected Member for the Uxbridge Division of Middlesex. He was a partner in the firm of Glyn, Mills, Currie & Company, Bankers.

He received his first commission in 1909, being appointed to the West Kent Yeomanry (Territorial Force). He was embodied on the outbreak of War and served with his unit at home until May 26th, 1915, when he was appointed to a commission as Second Lieutenant in the Special Reserve of Officers, Scots Guards.

On joining his new regiment he performed duty at home with the 3rd (Reserve) Battalion until he proceeded to join the British Expeditionary Force in France for service with the 2nd Battalion on June 12th, 1915. He fell in action at Hulluch on October 6th, 1915, and his name is perpetuated on the Loos Memorial.

An intimate friend has written of him:

"Charlie Mills was the finest character I have ever been fortunate enough to meet. A good man, a fine sportsman, with wonderful charm and spirits, everybody who came into contact with him loved him. Wherever he went he made friends at once; at Eton and Oxford, in his constituency, in the House of Commons, in the hunting-field, which he loved with all the passion of a bold and skilful horseman, in the City, and in these last months on the field of battle his pleasant and attractive personality carried him along so easily, that it was difficult for people who only knew him casually to realize what solid gifts of intellect as well as of heart he carried behind his high spirits and ready wit. Though still under 30 at the time of his death, he had already won for himself the respect of all parties in the House of Commons, and in the City his keen and clear-sighted judgment was well known to those whose opinions count.

"I have known no one of whom it could be more truly said that he was a great-hearted Christian gentleman."

CAPTAIN THE HON. A. E. B. O'NEILL

2nd Life Guards

ARTHUR EDWARD BRUCE O'NEILL, eldest surviving son of the 2nd Lord O'Neill, was born on September 19th, 1876. He was educated at Eton, having been in Mr. Luxmoore's house, and was in the boats. He was greatly valued for his amiable and stainlessly upright career. If he was less widely known, it was because his modesty and intelligence and sweet temper made less display of the vigour and firmness which he showed later, not only in the South African War and in his political life, but also in the patriotic organization of his native Ulster.

He was a Justice of the Peace and Deputy Lieutenant for County Antrim; was musical, a good shot and fond of all sports.

Captain O'Neill joined the 2nd Life Guards in 1897, and served with distinction in the South African War with the Composite Regiment of Household Cavalry, receiving the King's Medal and the Queen's Medal with three clasps. He was present at the Relief of Kimberley and at operations in the Orange Free State, at Paardeberg and in Cape Colony, including the actions of Driefontein and Colesberg. He was seconded for service in the House of Commons in 1910 and sat as Member for Mid-Antrim until his death.

He rejoined his regiment on the outbreak of War, proceeding overseas in October, 1914. He fell in action near Zwartelen on November 6th, 1914, on the occasion on which the Household Cavalry were used as infantry on one of the most critical days of the first battle of Ypres, while leading his men in a gallant attempt to save a situation. He was shot on Klein Zillebeke ridge, and, shouting to his men to line the ridge, was being carried out when he received another wound, and then begged his bearers to leave him and save themselves. He did not know what fear was. He saw his task accomplished. His name is perpetuated on the Menin Gate Memorial, Ypres.

Captain O'Neill was the first Member of the House of Commons to fall in the War.

CAPTAIN THE RT. HON. N. J. A. PRIMROSE, P.C., M.C.

Royal Bucks Hussars

NEIL JAMES ARCHIBALD PRIMROSE, second son of the 5th Earl of Rosebery, K.G. (Prime Minister 1894–5), was born on December 14th, 1882. He went to Eton with his brother, Lord Dalmeny, to Mr. Durnford's house in 1894 and left in 1899. Never very strong, he won no great success in athletics but made many friendships which he retained to the close of his life, and those who knew him best believed that he would make his mark in politics, a hope which was amply justified. On leaving Eton he went to New College, Oxford, and entered public life in 1909 as an Alderman of the London County Council. In January, 1910, he was elected Member for the Wisbech Division of Cambridgeshire, and, opposed by Lord Robert Cecil, retained his seat with a largely increased majority the following year. In the earlier months of 1914, when the Irish controversy was nearing its height, Mr. Primrose took an independent line, strongly criticizing the Government for not taking proceedings against those who were most actively associated with the landing of arms in Ulster.

On the outbreak of War, he at once rejoined his regiment and was engaged on military service until February, 1915, when he was brought back to the House of Commons to be Under-Secretary of State for Foreign Affairs. After a further period of military service, he was appointed, in the autumn of 1916, Parliamentary Military Secretary to the Ministry of Munitions, and joint Parliamentary Secretary to the Treasury; he was made a Privy Councillor in 1917. Later in the same year he returned to the front for the last time. He died of wounds received in action at the third Battle of Gaza, on November 18th, 1917, and was buried in Ramleh War Cemetery, Palestine.

Captain Primrose was awarded the Military Cross.

LIEUT. AND ADJT. THE VISCOUNT QUENINGTON

Royal Gloucestershire Hussars Yeomanry

MICHAEL HUGH HICKS-BEACH, VISCOUNT QUENINGTON, was the only son of the Rt. Hon. Sir Michael Hicks-Beach, Bart. (1st Earl St. Aldwyn), M.P. for E. Gloucestershire, 1864-85, and for Bristol West, 1885-1906, and Chancellor of the Exchequer, 1885-6 and 1895-1902.

He was born on January 19th, 1877, and was educated at Eton and Christ Church, Oxford.

Formerly a Captain in the 4th Battalion Gloucester Regiment (Militia) (disbanded in 1908), he served with it at St. Helena during the Boer War (1900-1), receiving the South African War Medal. He was elected Member of Parliament for the Tewkesbury Division of Gloucestershire in 1906. He later joined the Royal Gloucestershire Hussars Yeomanry and served with them through the Gallipoli Campaign and in Egypt. He was mortally wounded in action at Katia, Egypt, on April 23rd, 1916, and died before reaching hospital. He was buried in Cairo New British Protestant Cemetery.

Viscount Quenington was mentioned in despatches.

MAJOR W. H. K. REDMOND

Royal Irish Regiment

WILLIAM HOEY KEARNEY REDMOND, born April 13th, 1861, was the second son of William Archer Redmond, who himself sat for many years in the House of Commons as member for the borough of Wexford, with which town the family associations go back many years. He was educated at Clongowes Wood College, Co. Kildare, and became subsequently a lieutenant in the County Wexford Militia Battalion of the Royal Irish Regiment, intending to adopt the Army as a profession; but he resigned his commission to take part in the Land League Movement. After a year spent in Kilmainham Gaol as a consequence of his activities, he and his brother, Mr. John Redmond, were sent by Mr. Parnell on a mission to Australia to raise funds in support of the Nationalist movement. During his absence in Australia in 1883 he was nominated and returned for the borough of Wexford —defeating The O'Conor Don. He sat for Wexford until 1885, when he was returned for an Ulster constituency, County Fermanagh, and in 1892 for East Clare, which he continuously represented till the time of his death.

When War broke ou the instantly recognized that it was the duty of Ireland to take her full share in the struggle. After training at Aldershot with the Irish Division—though then 54 years of age—he received in February, 1915, a commission as Captain in the Royal Irish Regiment, in which he had served 33 years previously, and left with it for the front on December 16th, 1915. He was present at the capture of Guillemont by the Irish Division.

Major Redmond was wounded at Wytschaete Ridge in the Battle of Messines on June 7th, 1917; he died the same day and was buried in the garden of Locre Hospice.

For his services at the front he was promoted Major, mentioned in despatches and awarded the Legion of Honour.

His Majesty the King telegraphed to Mr. John Redmond, M.P.:

"Buckingham Palace.

"I am grieved to hear of the death from wounds received in action of your brother, Major Redmond, who has given gallant service and a noble example in the war. I heartily sympathize with you and his family in your loss.—GEORGE R.I."

Speaking of him in the House of Commons, the Prime Minister, Mr. Lloyd George, said: "There were political tasks at home which his genial presence, his great personal popularity, and his moving powers of speech would have been useful to aid. He elected instead to face death on the battle-field."

LIEUT.-COL. LORD A. G. B. THYNNE, D.S.O.

Royal Wiltshire Yeomanry

ALEXANDER GEORGE BOTEVILLE THYNNE was the third and youngest son of the 4th Marquess of Bath. Born on February 17th, 1873, he was educated at Eton and Balliol College, Oxford. After unsuccessfully contesting the Frome Division in the Unionist interest in 1896 and Bath in January, 1906, he was elected one of the members for Bath in January, 1910, and he represented that city up to the time of his death. He became a member of the London County Council in 1899, sitting for the City of London until the following year. Since 1910 he had represented East Marylebone on the Council. Lord Alexander, who was a major in the Yeomanry and honorary lieutenant in the Army, served in the South African War with the 1st Battalion Imperial Yeomanry, being on the Staff in 1900–1902, and receiving both medals with five clasps. From 1902 to 1905 he was secretary to the Lieutenant-Governor of the Orange River Colony, and in 1903–1904 accompanied the Somaliland Field Force as Reuter's special correspondent, being awarded the medal with clasp.

On the outbreak of the present War he was in camp with the Wilts Yeomanry, of which he was in command. He went to the front as second in command of a battalion of the Worcester Regiment, but later received the command of a battalion of the Wilts Regiment, being afterwards transferred to another Wilts battalion, with which he was serving when he fell. Lord Alexander, who was twice wounded, in July, 1916, during the Battle of the Somme, and again in April, 1918, fell in action on Sept. 14th, 1918, and was buried in Béthune Town Cemetery.

He was awarded the D.S.O. and the Croix de Guerre, and was mentioned in despatches.

LIEUT. THE HON. W. L. C. WALROND

Royal Army Service Corps

WILLIAM LIONEL CHARLES WALROND was the only surviving son of the 1st Lord Waleran, formerly Sir William Walrond, M.P. for the Tiverton Division of Devon. He was born on May 22nd, 1876, and was educated privately and abroad. He was an accomplished linguist, speaking French, German, Italian and Spanish.

He was private secretary to his father when Chief Conservative Whip, and later acted in the same capacity to Sir Alexander Acland-Hood, when he succeeded Sir William Walrond in that office.

In 1907, on the elevation of his father to the Peerage, Mr. Walrond succeeded him in the representation of the Tiverton Division of Devon, fighting three elections and doubling his majority on each occasion.

In 1914-15 he was employed as Railway Transport Officer between Le Havre and the front and died on November 3rd, 1915, from consumption of the throat contracted in France as the result of exposure. He was buried in Bradfield Churchyard, Uffculme, Devon.

III.

OFFICERS
OF THE
HOUSE OF COMMONS

LIEUT. R. N. M. BAILEY

East Riding of Yorkshire Yeomanry

ROBERT NEALE MENTETH BAILEY, only son of Henry Bailey, Esquire, J.P., D.L., Coates, Cirencester, by his second wife Christina Thomson, was born on August 21st, 1882. He was educated at Eton, where he was King's Scholar, and at Magdalen College, Oxford. He was elected to a Demyship at Magdalen in December, 1900, and took a First Class in Classical Moderations in 1903 and a Second Class in Literae Humaniores in 1905, becoming subsequently an Assistant Clerk in the Department of the Clerk of the House of Commons.

Lieut. Bailey was a good sportsman, fond of hunting, fishing and shooting. It was characteristic of him that, for fear of growing soft in a sheltered life, he went to Canada in 1913, to work as a labourer during the harvest season, and this proved a good training for the War which so soon followed.

One of those rare personalities loved by rich and poor alike, he was a scholar who turned to practical account his belief in education as a means of pleasure to the individual and as a factor in progress towards social betterment. In proof of this, the years devoted in his leisure time to the work of the Working Men's College at St. Pancras stand out in high relief. "Gentleness in all things," they wrote of him, "was his striking characteristic, but self-sacrifice was a part of his nature. At the call of duty he gave up at once all he had worked for, since, for him, his country's need was paramount."

He joined the East Yorkshire Yeomanry from the Inns of Court O.T.C. in August, 1914, and went to Egypt in September, 1915. While serving in the Egyptian Campaign he was wounded at Naane, in Palestine, on November 14th, 1917, and died a fortnight later at Cairo, on December 1st, 1917. He was buried in the Cairo War Memorial Cemetery.

On his military duties he carried with him always Thackeray's Greek Anthology stripping off first the cover and then the less precious pages lest it should interfere with military necessities.

In his regiment, as elsewhere, Lieut. Bailey was loved by all. His squadron leader wrote:

"No one could wish for a better man to be with in a scrap, he was as brave as the best, and stuck out the long and boring hardships we have had with the best of hearts. I think he was literally the most popular officer in the regiment."

SECOND LIEUT. R. W. T. COX

6th Battalion Dorset Regiment

ROBERT WILLIAM TALBOT COX, eldest son of George Talbot Cox, Esquire, of Knight's Hill, Norwood, Surrey, was born on May 28th, 1890. He was educated at Merchant Taylors' School, where he was Head Monitor, and proceeded thence by open Classical Scholarship to New College, Oxford, becoming later an Assistant Clerk in the Department of the Clerk of the House of Commons. He enlisted as a private in the 15th London Regiment (Civil Service Rifles) the day following the declaration of War and proceeded with it to France, taking part in engagements at Neuve Chapelle, Festubert and Lòos throughout 1915. In December, 1915, he obtained a commission in the 6th Dorset Regiment, a county with which his family had long been associated. He was commended for conspicuous gallantry, having gone out early in the morning of February 15th, 1916, under machine gun and rifle fire in an endeavour to rescue a private of the Lincolnshire Regiment. In so doing he received wounds from which he died the same day. He was buried in Spoilbank Cemetery, Zillebeke.

Sir Courtenay Ilbert, Clerk of the House of Commons, wrote of him:

"During the short period of his service in the Clerk's Department he had gained the affection and esteem of his colleagues."

Lieut. Cox was mentioned in despatches.

LIEUT. V. W. D. FOX

Irish Guards

VICTOR WILLIAM DARWIN FOX, son of Gerard Fox, Esquire, J.P. (Hants), Hythe, Southampton, was born on May 31st, 1883. He entered Bradfield College in September, 1897, and became a Prefect in 1901, proceeding to Wadham College, Oxford, as an Exhibitioner in 1902. After taking his degree in 1905, he passed 76th in the Entrance Examination for the Indian Civil Service in 1906, and became an Assistant Clerk in the Department of the Clerk of the House of Commons in 1907.

His interests lay mainly in music, pictures and travel abroad. He inherited from his father a love for collecting, and his own taste and feeling for "objects" were singularly keen. His was a very gentle nature and his unfailing courtesy had an old-fashioned quality which was rare, even before the War.

He joined the Inns of Court O.T.C. on October 6th, 1914, having acted as Speaker's Secretary for a time until he joined the Irish Guards himself. Having obtained a commission, he proceeded to France on February 3rd, 1915, and served in the trenches for three months. He fell in action at Festubert on May 18th, 1915, and was buried in Le Touret Military Cemetery, Richebourg-l'Avoué.

MAJOR H. S. GREEN

7th Battalion London Regiment

HORACE SALKELD GREEN, son of Charles Thomas Green, Esquire, Banker, was born on January 25th, 1883. He was educated at Harrow where he was Entrance Scholar in 1897; Monitor, and Clayton Scholar in 1901, and Roundell Scholar in 1902. He was also in the Shooting VIII and Captain of it in 1902. He went on to Trinity College, Cambridge, where he was Science Scholar in 1902, and was in the University Shooting VIII and IV from 1903 to 1905.

A weak heart, due to rheumatic fever in boyhood, had thwarted his ambition to enter the Army on leaving school. He was, however, in the Inns of Court O.T.C. from 1905 to 1910, and received a commission in the 7th Battalion London Regiment in October, 1910, being promoted Captain in September, 1914, and Major in September, 1917; the notice of this last promotion to the substantive rank of Major did not appear, however, till after his death.

He was an Assistant Clerk in the Department of the Clerk of the House of Commons.

He was mobilized on August 4th, 1914, but, on account of ill health, was transferred to the 2/7th Battalion of his Regiment in December, and acted as Adjutant of it until his transfer to the command of a Company. He proceeded overseas in January, 1917, and was in action at Bullecourt and Passchendaele. He was instantaneously killed at Poelcapelle on September 20th, 1917, while in command of the two forward Companies of his regiment during the phase of the third Battle of Ypres, which began on that date. He was buried in Tyne Cot Cemetery, Passchendaele.

Major Green was mentioned in despatches.

CORPORAL R. LANCHBERY

8th Royal Highlanders (Black Watch)

REGINALD LANCHBERY, son of William Lanchbery, formerly house painter in the employment of His Majesty's Office of Works, was born on August 7th, 1892. He was educated at Elsenham Street Council School, Wandsworth, where he gained a Medal for Cricket and a Certificate for Swimming.

At the time of the outbreak of War he was employed as a sessional cleaner in the department of the Serjeant-at-Arms, House of Commons.

He enlisted in the Black Watch on December 7th, 1914, and proceeded overseas the following May. He was present at the Battle of Loos in September, 1915, and in all the other engagements in which the regiment took part from the time of landing until he fell in action at the Battle of the Somme on July 17th, 1916. He was buried in La Neuville British Cemetery, Corbie.

SECOND LIEUT. W. K. SANDERSON

1st Battalion Border Regiment

WALTER KER SANDERSON, only surviving son of the late Dr. Sanderson, of Penrith, was born on August 19th, 1881. He was educated at Sedbergh School. On leaving school he studied medicine at Edinburgh University for three years, but, having no taste for it, he entered the Vote Office at the House of Commons in 1906.

During his London life he was keenly interested in social work, living for some years at Toynbee Hall in the East End.

He had intended to stand for Parliament in later life as he was an excellent debater, full of wit and humour and quick at repartee.

On the outbreak of War he enlisted in the Public Schools Battalion, and was gazetted later to the Queen's Own Royal West Kent Regiment. He brooked no delay, however, and went out to the front in August, 1915, as a private in the H.A.C. In the following year he was given a commission in the Border Regiment, taking part in the first and second Battles of Ypres, and it was on July 1st, 1916, while bravely leading his men into the thickest of the action on the first day of the Battle of the Somme, that he fell. His name is perpetuated on the Thiepval Memorial.

A brother officer wrote:

"It may be some comfort to know that he died as gallant a death as any officer or man could. He was leading his platoon right up to the German lines, and never faltered or checked when caught by the terrible fire. His loss is a very serious one to the regiment."

LIEUT. F. SEYMOUR

7th Battalion King's Royal Rifle Corps

FRANCIS SEYMOUR, second son of Hugh Francis Seymour, Esquire, Potterells, Hatfield, Herts, was born on May 30th, 1886. He was educated at Eton and Trinity College, Cambridge. Though not attaining to any great distinction in sport, he was fond of it in all forms, particularly grouse shooting and deer-stalking. An Assistant Clerk in the Department of the Clerk of the House of Commons, he had many friends. Joining the Inns of Court O.T.C. in August, 1914, he subsequently obtained a commission in the King's Royal Rifle Corps. He proceeded to France with his regiment in May, 1915, and fell in action at Hooge on July 30th following in a severe action in which his trench became most difficult to hold.

His Commanding Officer, in describing the circumstances of his death and the loss to the regiment, wrote:

"I had tried to be as careful as possible with him always on account of his height (6ft. 6in.), but on this occasion we were heavily attacked and we counter-attacked and lost heavily in officers and men. He was a universal favourite and was making an excellent soldier."

Similar tributes from brother officers testify to his worth. Invaluable in the Company and very popular with his men, all felt the loss of "this splendid English gentleman who has shared our discomforts, our jokes and serious moments from the inception of the Battalion"— one of them wrote of him.

His name is perpetuated on the Menin Gate Memorial, Ypres.

IV.

SONS
OF
MEMBERS
OF THE
HOUSE OF COMMONS

LANCE-CORPORAL J. C. ADAMSON

7th Seaforth Highlanders

JAMES CUNNINGHAM ADAMSON was born at Halbeath, in the County of Fife, on April 2nd, 1893. He was the eldest son of the Rt. Hon. Wm. Adamson, M.P. for West Fife, LL.D. of St Andrews University, Secretary for Scotland, and a Member of the Cabinet in the first Labour Government, in 1924, and again in 1929.

He received his early education at the public school at Halbeath, and later at Queen Anne School, Dunfermline. At school he entered keenly into all athletic sports, particularly football, and swimming, for which he won several prizes. On leaving school he became a student at Skerry's College, Edinburgh, and was thereafter for a short time in a Law Office in Dunfermline, later receiving an appointment with the Scottish Miners' Federation Approved Society, Glasgow. There his ability soon earned recognition and before long he was promoted to the position of Assistant General Secretary of that Organization.

When War broke out he enlisted as a private in the 10th Battalion Seaforth Highlanders, and on being sent to France was transferred to the 7th Battalion. While serving in that regiment he was promoted Lance-Corporal, and arrangements had been made for his promotion to commissioned rank, but before this could be carried out he was killed during an attack which his battalion made on Butte de Warlencourt on October 12th, 1916.

His name is perpetuated on the Thiepval Memorial.

LIEUT. J. S. AINSWORTH

11th (Prince Albert's Own) Hussars

JOHN STIRLING AINSWORTH, second son of Sir John S. Ainsworth, Bart., M.P. for Argyllshire, 1903-18, was born on November 9th, 1889. He was educated at Eton and Sandhurst. He joined the 11th Hussars in April, 1909, was promoted Lieutenant in 1911, and went out with the Expeditionary Force in August, 1914. He was killed while on Patrol duty near Merris on October 13th, 1914, and was buried in Méteren Military Cemetery.

Lieut. Ainsworth was mentioned in Sir John French's despatch of the 8th October, 1914.

LIEUT.-COL. D. K. ANDERSON, M.C.

Machine Gun Corps

DONALD KNOX ANDERSON, second son of George Knox Anderson, Esquire, D.L., and M.P. for Canterbury City, was born on May 11th, 1886. He was educated at King's School, Canterbury, where he was in the Cricket XI and the Football XV, playing later for the Kent Amateurs, "The Band of Brothers" Cricket Club.

He had served with the 2nd Battalion Royal West Kent Regiment since 1908, and was at home on leave from India when the War broke out. He was attached to the 6th Battalion when raised for training and went overseas in May, 1915, as Brigade Machine Gun Officer, serving as Division and Corps Machine Gun Officer. He was killed in the Cambrai Sector by a chance shell on December 3rd, 1917, when handing over his position on returning home to a Staff appointment with the Machine Gun Corps at Grantham. His name is perpetuated on the Cambrai Memorial.

Colonel Anderson was several times mentioned in despatches and awarded the Military Cross.

LIEUT. C. K. ANDERSON

The Queen's Own (Royal West Kent) Regiment

COLIN KNOX ANDERSON, born July 22nd, 1888, whose name appeared in the first list of British losses issued by the War Office, was the third son of George Knox Anderson, Esquire, D.L., and M.P. for Canterbury City. He was educated at Malvern College where he was a School Prefect and in the Cricket and the Football XI. He was good at all games, but chiefly excelled at Cricket, being well-known in regimental Cricket and with the Kent Amateurs—"The Band of Brothers." When War was declared he was employed on civil work at Rochester, but at once offered his services, which were accepted. He had served with the 3rd Battalion of his regiment for several years before the War but joined the 1st Battalion on mobilization and proceeded with it to France.

He fell in action on August 23rd, 1914, at St. Ghislain on the Condé Canal, and was buried in Hautrage Military Cemetery.

CAPTAIN THE HON. ARTHUR ANNESLEY

10th Royal (Prince of Wales's Own) Hussars

ARTHUR ANNESLEY, eldest son of the 11th Viscount Valentia in the Peerage of Ireland, M.P. for Oxford City 1895-1917, and 1st Baron Annesley, was born on August 24th, 1880. He was educated at Eton and received his commission in the 10th Royal Hussars from the 3rd (Militia) Oxfordshire and Buckinghamshire Light Infantry in April, 1900. He served with his regiment in the South African War from 1900 to 1902, being present at operations in the Transvaal and Cape Colony for which he received the Queen's Medal with three clasps and the King's Medal with two clasps. He also received the Coronation Medal of King George V. Having obtained his Captaincy in 1907, he served as Adjutant of his regiment from May, 1907, to December, 1908, and, in November, 1912, was appointed A.D.C. to the General Officer commanding in Egypt, an appointment he was holding when War broke out.

He was killed in action by a sniper at Zillebeke on November 16th, 1914, and was buried in Ypres Town Cemetery.

LIEUT. D. M. ARCHDALE

1st King's African Rifles

DOMINIC MERVYN ARCHDALE, fourth son of the Rt. Hon. E. M. Archdale, M.P. for North Fermanagh, was born on April 4th, 1892. He was educated at Felstead School and Wye Agricultural College, and was in the Football and Hockey XI at both. He took the College Diploma in Agriculture at Wye and in September, 1913, was appointed by the Colonial Office Assistant Agriculturist in Nyasaland with charge of the Experimental Farm.

On the outbreak of War he joined the Machine Gun Corps Colonial Force and took part in the first engagement at Keronga. He transferred later to the King's African Rifles and fell in action at Lupembe, German East Africa, on November 13th, 1916.

He was buried in Iringa Cemetery.

LIEUT. RAYMOND ASQUITH

Grenadier Guards

RAYMOND ASQUITH, eldest son of the Rt. Hon. Herbert Henry Asquith, K.C., M.P. for East Fife, 1886-1918, Paisley, 1920, and Prime Minister 1908-16, 1st Earl of Oxford and Asquith (1925), was born on November 6th, 1878. He was educated at Winchester where he won the Queen's Gold Medal for Latin Essay, together with the Warden and Fellows' Prizes for Greek Prose and Verse, and in 1897 was awarded the Goddard Scholarship. He was also second Captain of College VI, and in this same year Prefect of Chapel. He then went up with a Scholarship to Balliol College, Oxford, where he had an exceptionally fine career. He took First Classes in Classical Moderations, Literæ Humaniores and Jurisprudence and was awarded successively the Craven, Ireland, Derby and Eldon Scholarships. In 1900 he was elected President of the Union and, in 1901, a Fellow of All Souls. In 1904 he was called to the Bar by the Inner Temple and had laid the foundations of a large practice. He was engaged as Junior Counsel in the North Atlantic Arbitration and in the inquiry into the loss of the *Titanic*. Shortly before the War he was appointed a Junior Counsel to the Board of Inland Revenue and adopted as prospective Liberal Candidate for Derby. Soon after War broke out he was gazetted to the Queen's Westminsters, whence he transferred later to the Grenadier Guards. For a time he was employed on the staff, but at his own urgent request was sent back to his battalion a few weeks before the opening of the Battle of the Somme. He fell in Trônes Wood on September 15th, 1916, and was buried in Guillemont Road Cemetery.

Lieut. Asquith was mentioned in despatches.

SECOND LIEUT. A. S. BALFOUR

Royal Field Artillery

ALAN SCOTT BALFOUR, younger son of Sir Robert Balfour, Bart., M.P. for Partick Division of Glasgow, was born on May 22nd, 1894. He was educated at Harrow and Trinity College, Oxford, and later entered the office of Messrs. Balfour, Williamson & Co., Merchants. He joined the Artists' Rifles early in 1916 and obtained a commission in the Royal Field Artillery the following August, proceeding to France in October. He returned home in July, 1917, for training as observer in the Royal Flying Corps and went back on appointment as observation officer in September. He was killed in action while on Photographic Reconnaissance of the enemy's lines on January 13th, 1918, and was buried in Tincourt New British Cemetery.

CAPTAIN C. W. BANBURY

Coldstream Guards

CHARLES WILLIAM BANBURY, only son of the Rt. Hon. Sir Frederick George Banbury, Bart., M.P. for the City of London from 1906 until his elevation to the Peerage in 1924, was born on February 11th, 1877. He was at Eton from 1890-95, and boarded at Miss Evans'. He went on to University College, Oxford, where he rowed in his College Four and Eight, and joined the Coldstream Guards in August, 1899.

He soon saw active service in the South African War, during which he took part in operations in Cape Colony, the Transvaal and the Orange River Colony in 1900, and in further operations in Cape Colony in 1901-2. For his services he received the Queen's Medal with three clasps, and the King's Medal with two clasps. He was appointed A.D.C. to the General Officer Commanding the First Division, Aldershot Command, in 1909.

An excellent and remarkably successful rider, he won, while at Aldershot, the Grand Military Steeplechase twice, and the Aldershot Cup, the Coldstream Guards' Plate and the Household Brigade Cup, each three times.

In 1912 he was appointed A.D.C. to the General Officer Commanding-in-Chief, Eastern Command, and was with that officer (Lieut.-General Sir J. M. Grierson) when he died suddenly in France in August, 1914. He accompanied the General's body to England, and attended the military funeral at Glasgow, returning to France on August 23rd to rejoin his regiment.

He was twice wounded in action on September 14th, died two days later at Soupir, near Soissons, and was buried in Soupir Communal Cemetery.

From the circumstances in which Captain Banbury met his death, it appears that the Germans hoisted the White Flag and had a body of infantry in concealment, so that when our men advanced on seeing the White Flag, they were exposed to the oblique fire of this body.

An officer, who served under him wrote of the grief of the whole battalion, adding that "he was extraordinarily brave and handled his Company beautifully."

Many friends who spoke of him affectionately as "Cakes" will readily think of the happy combination in him of natural grace, fearlessness and unforgettable charm.

SECOND LIEUT. H. BARNES

2nd Gordon Highlanders

HENRY BARNES, younger son of the Rt. Hon. George Nicoll Barnes, C.H., M.P. for Blackfriars (Gorbals) Division of Glasgow (1906), was born on May 23rd, 1889. He was educated at the Goldsmith (Peckham Road) Elementary School and the Borough Polytechnic, specializing in languages. After several years spent in the London City and Midland Bank, he obtained an appointment in the Bank of Spain.

On the outbreak of War he joined the Seaforth Highlanders and went to France in November, 1914, being subsequently promoted 2nd lieutenant in the field in March, 1915.

He fell in action, while in an advanced position at Hulluch, in the Battle of Loos, on September 25th, 1915, and was buried in Dud Corner Cemetery, Loos.

CAPTAIN R. N. BARRAN

2nd Life Guards

ROWLAND NOEL BARRAN, eldest son of Sir John Barran, Bart., M.P. for Leeds North, 1902-18, was born on December 25th, 1887, and was educated at Repton. He was for some years Lieutenant in the 1st West Riding Royal Field Artillery. He joined the 11th Hussars in September, 1914, and was transferred to the 2nd Life Guards, proceeding with them to France in October, 1915. After being invalided home in April, 1917, he acted as A.D.C. to General Sir Francis Lloyd, returning again to France in the spring of 1918. He died on March 13th, 1919, while on his way to Constantinople to join the Staff of General Bridges, and was buried in Windsor (Spital) Cemetery, Berkshire.

SECOND LIEUT. E. A. BEAUCHAMP

Coldstream Guards

EDWARD ARCHIBALD BEAUCHAMP, elder son of Sir Edward Beauchamp, Bart., M.P. for the Lowestoft Division of Suffolk, was born on April 5th, 1891, and was educated at Eton, where he had his House football colours, and at Trinity Hall, Cambridge. He also studied in Germany and France, passing second in French in his examination for the Army. He joined the Special Reserve of the Coldstream Guards in February, 1914, and left for the front with the 3rd Battalion in September. He was with his battalion in the open fighting round St. Julien which led up to the Battle of Ypres. There were heavy casualties in his platoon at Polygon Wood, he himself being wounded on November 1st. He returned to England, and, on his recovery, joined the 1st Battalion and was with it in the advance on Givenchy, where he fell mortally wounded on December 21st, 1914, dying the following day at Lillers, near Béthune. He was buried in Lillers Communal Cemetery.

Lieut. Beauchamp earned the highest praise from his superiors, who speak of his keenness, initiative and gallantry. Every one testified to his bravery and coolness, and there can be no question for anyone who heard him speaking of his experiences, that in the Army he had found his true *métier*, and that, had he been spared, he would have displayed the same ability in the higher ranks that he had already shown as a subaltern. A cheerful and unassuming boy at Eton, he ended his life still cheerful and unassuming, and a man trusted alike by superiors, equals and subordinates—for he was brave, simple-hearted and straightforward.

SECOND LIEUT. F. H. BETHELL

3rd Connaught Rangers

FRANK HARRY BETHELL, eldest son of Sir John Henry Bethell, Bart., M.P. for the Romford Division of Essex, 1906-18, and subsequently for East Ham North, until his elevation to the Peerage in 1922, was born on May 18th, 1896. He was educated at Harrow, where he was Captain of the Small Houses at football and a Member of the School O.T.C., and at Trinity College, Cambridge. He joined the Connaught Rangers in September, 1914, and proceeded overseas the following March. He was officially reported missing after the Battle of Loos but was later found to have fallen in action on September 25th, 1915, whilst leading his Platoon.

His name is perpetuated on the Menin Gate Memorial, Ypres.

SECOND LIEUT. H. F. BOLES

17th Lancers (attached Royal Flying Corps)

HASTINGS FORTESCUE BOLES, eldest son of Lieut.-Colonel Sir Dennis F. Boles, C.B.E. (Baronet, 1922), M.P. for West Somerset, 1911, and the Taunton Division, 1918-21, was born on June 21st, 1895. He was educated at Eton and Sandhurst. At School he did not rise to any special distinction, but he knew what was meant by playing a hard, clean game of football. In the summer of 1914 he passed into Sandhurst, where in the Cavalry Company he was considered a specially good rider. In due course he was gazetted to the 17th Lancers; but while at Sandhurst he had volunteered for the Flying Corps, and in March, 1915, he was recalled from his regiment at the Curragh and sent out to France as an observer. Absolutely fearless, he at once made his mark in the new capacity, excelling particularly in the photographs he took over the enemy lines. Cool and quick in his work, he was considered by his superiors an observer of no ordinary type; while his piano-playing made many a monotonous hour seem shorter to the members of his Flight.

He was carrying out a reconnaissance on May 24th, 1915, when he was struck by a piece of shell which went through his head. Turning round to his pilot he smiled and waved his hand, and he even managed to get out of the aeroplane himself, although he can hardly have still been conscious. He passed away the same evening and was buried in Bailleul Communal Cemetery Extension.

His squadron commander wrote to his father:

"I am having these last photographs he took re-done, to send you when the War is over, as they are splendid examples of his skill and bravery. He was by far the best at photography in the air that this squadron or any squadron is likely to produce."

LIEUT. H. J. BOYTON

Grenadier Guards

HENRY JAMES BOYTON, born on February 21st, 1892, was the only son of Sir James Boyton, J.P. County of London, and M.P. for East Marylebone, 1910-18. He was educated at Harrow and Jesus College, Cambridge. At Cambridge he rowed for the Jesus 1st Boat, Head of the River, 1912, and in the Henley Regatta of 1914 rowed bow in the 2nd Eight, which was runner-up in the final for the Thames Challenge Cup. He was also a member of the Marlow and London Rowing Clubs.

Lieutenant Boyton took a commission while still at Cambridge in the 1st City of London Royal Fusiliers, and was promoted Lieutenant in January, 1914. Soon after the outbreak of War he went to Malta with his regiment and returned with them to France in March, 1915. He was wounded at Festubert on May 9th, 1915, and on his recovery was posted to a Reserve Battalion of his regiment, in which he became Captain and Adjutant. In July, 1916, he transferred to the Grenadier Guards and left for the front the following October. He was killed in action on the night of December 14th, 1916, at Sailly-Saillisel on the Somme, and was buried in Combles Communal Cemetery Extension.

His Colonel wrote:

"He was a most gallant and lovable personality, and his loss is much felt by all ranks."

SUB-LIEUT. W. P. BRACE

Royal Naval Volunteer Reserve

WILLIAM PERCY BRACE, elder son of the Rt. Hon. William Brace, M.P. for Glamorgan South, 1906-18, and for the Abertillery Division of Monmouth from 1918, Parliamentary Under Secretary of State, Home Department, 1915-18, was born on April 13th, 1892. He was educated at Llandovery College and Aberdeen University. Before the War he was employed at the Board of Agriculture and Fisheries and, later, at the Ministry of Munitions. He joined the Royal Fusiliers in 1917, and in 1918 obtained a commission in the Royal Naval Volunteer Reserve.

He died from pneumonia, while on service, at the Royal Naval Hospital, Chatham, on October 23rd, 1918, and was buried in Newport (St. Woolos) Cemetery, Monmouthshire.

SECOND LIEUT. G. C. BRASSEY

Coldstream Guards

GERARD CHARLES BRASSEY, second son of Major Leonard Brassey, M.P. for the Peterborough Division of Northamptonshire, was born on December 28th, 1898. He was educated at Wellington House, Westgate-on-Sea, and at Eton, where he was Captain of the Oppidans in 1917.

He went to the front in March and fell in action near St. Léger on August 27th, 1918, following. He was buried in Mory Street Military Cemetery, St. Léger.

Though he came to no great athletic eminence, there were few at Eton who did not know Gerard Brassey. His varied interests and abilities made him a delightful companion; in his last year he gave great intellectual promise, and, had he survived the War, would certainly have brought honour to his School in other fields. As Captain of his House, he showed fine moral strength and won the confidence of all; and those who had observed this closely were not surprised at the courage in battle displayed by one who seemed externally so gentle. They think of him now as a splendid example of the high moral qualities which are fostered by a liberal education. All the prizes he might have won he surrendered at the call of duty; and all that he owed to Eton he has repaid with the inestimable sacrifice.

SECOND LIEUT. A. H. ROSDEW BURN

Royal Dragoons

ARTHUR HERBERT ROSDEW BURN, born on June 30th, 1892, was the eldest son of Colonel Charles Rosdew Burn (later Sir Charles Forbes-Leith, Bart.) M.P. for the Torquay Division of Devon, A.D.C. to the King, and grandson of Lord Leith of Fyvie. He was educated at Eton, where he was in the Upper Boats, and at Christ Church, Oxford, where he was a Member of Bullingdon. He hunted regularly, and was a good shot and a keen fisherman.

Lieut. Burn was at Eton from September, 1905, to July, 1909. He left early, to the sorrow of all who knew him, in order to spend several months in Germany, learning the language, before proceeding to Oxford. Thanks to this he was appointed Interpreter to his Brigadier, but at the last moment was ordered to take out the first reinforcements to his regiment, the 1st Royal Dragoons. He was singularly sweet-tempered, full of that large charity which endeavours to find some good in every one. A giant in stature, and very powerful, he had in a marked degree the gentleness and simple-minded fidelity often found with great physical strength.

He obtained a commission as a University candidate on August 16th, 1914, and served in the trenches at the first Battle of Ypres in September. He fell in action at the Château of Hollebeke on October 30th, 1914, when his regiment was ordered to retire from the trenches they were occupying.

His name is perpetuated on the Menin Gate Memorial Ypres.

LIEUT. COMMANDER P. S. CAMPBELL

Drake Battalion, Royal Naval Division

PHILIP SIDNEY CAMPBELL, youngest son of the Rt. Hon. James H. Campbell, M.P. for Dublin University, 1903-16 (later Lord Chancellor of Ireland and 1st Lord Glenavy, created 1921), was born on February 5th, 1893. He was educated at Thangways School, Dublin, and H.M.S. *Worcester*. He served in the Antwerp Expedition, and in Gallipoli, where he was wounded, and in France.

He fell in action at Beaumont Hamel, France, when taking over command of the Battalion on November 13th, 1916, after his Commanding Officer had been killed. He was buried in Ancre British Cemetery, Beaumont Hamel.

Lieut. Commander Campbell was three times mentioned in despatches.

SECOND LIEUT. F. L. CAREW

20th Hussars

FRANCIS LUDOVIC CAREW, second son of Charles R. S. Carew, Esquire, M.P. for the Tiverton Division of Devon, was born on March 4th, 1895. He was educated at Winchester, where he was appointed a House Prefect his last year (1912) and played in Commoner XV, and stood on Dress for VI, and at the Royal Military College, Sandhurst. He received a commission in the 20th Hussars on March 24th, 1914. He went to France with the 1st Division of the Expeditionary Force in August, 1914, and was killed in the trenches at Oosttaverne, near Ypres, by a sniper on October 30th, 1914.

His name is perpetuated on the Menin Gate Memorial, Ypres.

MAJOR E. H. H. CARLILE

Hertfordshire Yeomanry (attd. Hertfordshire Regiment)

EDWARD HILDRED HANBURY CARLILE, only son of Colonel Sir Hildred Carlile, Bart., C.B.E., M.P. for St. Albans Division of Hertfordshire, 1906-1919, was born on January 28th, 1881. He was educated at Harrow and Trinity College, Cambridge, boxing successfully as a feather-weight for his University against Oxford. He was a lieutenant in the Yorkshire Dragoons, a barrister of the Inner Temple, and from 1906 to 1914 was engaged in farming in Canada. He joined the Army in September, 1914, and proceeded overseas on January 18th, 1918. He was killed in action two months later, at Villers Faucon, near Peronne, while leading a forlorn hope on March 22nd, 1918.

His name is perpetuated on the Arras Memorial.

SECOND LIEUT. D. A. CARNEGIE

Royal Field Artillery

DAVID ALEXANDER CARNEGIE, second son of Lieut.-Col. the Hon. Douglas Carnegie, M.P. for Winchester, 1916-18, and grandson of the 9th Earl of Northesk, was born on January 15th, 1897. He was educated at Greshams School, Holt, Norfolk, and instead of going to Cambridge, as was intended, went to Woolwich. He received a commission in May, 1916, and was immediately sent out to France, where he took part in the engagements at Mametz and Contalmaison. He was killed in action by the explosion of an enemy shell in his battery at Brielen, near Ypres, on the 2nd of April, 1917, and was buried in Ferme-Oliver Military Cemetery at Elverdinghe, in Flanders.

The Colonel commanding his Brigade wrote:

"He was a splendidly gallant fellow who has done magnificent work always. He could always be absolutely depended upon, and his powers of observation and intuition were exceptional—his reports were always valuable.

"Both officers and men were most awfully fond of him."

MAJOR J. S. CAWLEY

20th Hussars

JOHN STEPHEN CAWLEY, third son of Sir Frederick Cawley, Bart., M.P. for the Prestwich Division of Lancashire, was born on the 27th October, 1879.

He was educated at Rugby and Sandhurst. He obtained his commission in the 20th Hussars in 1898, joining them at Mhow, India. He became Lieutenant in January, 1900, and obtained his troop in October, 1906. He served in the South African War, going to the Cape in 1901, where he was Signalling Officer to General Lowe's column. He was present at operations in Orange River Colony and Cape Colony and received the Queen's Medal with four clasps. He subsequently qualified as Second Class Interpreter in French, and served in Egypt, where he became Adjutant of his regiment.

Having passed through the Staff College he became Instructor at the Cavalry School at Netheravon in 1911, and in 1912 was appointed a General Staff Officer at the War Office. In 1913 he was appointed Brigade Major of the 1st Cavalry Brigade at Aldershot, and accompanied it to France in 1914.

Major Cawley was a good all round sportsman; he was in the Football XV and shooting VIII at Sandhurst; and in the Hockey team, and whip to the Drag at the Staff College. He played for his regiment at Polo when they won the Inter-regimental Cup in India (Meerut)

1901; the Clements Polo Cup in South Africa (Pretoria) 1903, and the Inter-regimental Cup (Hurlingham) 1906 and 1907. He won the Officers' riding and jumping prize at the Royal Military Tournament in 1905, and was well known with the North Hereford and Whaddon Chase Hunts.

Major Cawley was killed in action in the retirement from Mons on the 1st September, 1914, and was buried in Néry Communal Cemetery.

A brother officer gave the following account of his death:

"Our Brigade was attacked soon after dawn at Néry by a force double our number—a Cavalry Division with twelve guns. Owing to thick mist they managed to get within 600 yards of us; 350 horses of the Bays stampeded and their men went after them, and the "L" Battery R.H.A. was cut to pieces. The occasion was one which called for personal example, and Major Cawley, by permission of the General, went to help to restore order and get the broken remnants in their places. The situation being met and everyone being in his place, he joined the advanced line and was almost immediately killed by a piece of shell.

"The splendid manner in which he met his death in deliberately facing the awful fire to help others, when he really need not have done so, is only what his whole life had led us to expect."

His elder brother, Captain H. T. Cawley, M.P., and his younger brother, Captain the Hon. Oswald Cawley, M.P., also fell in action, and are commemorated elsewhere in this volume.

CAPTAIN R. G. H. CHALONER

3rd Battalion Wiltshire Regiment, and later 16th Lancers

RICHARD GODOLPHIN HUME CHALONER, eldest son of Colonel Chaloner, M.P. for the Abercromby Division of Liverpool from 1910, until his elevation to the Peerage in 1917 as 1st Baron Gisborough, was born on June 29th, 1883. He was educated at Eton, was in the 16th Lancers (1901-2), and was Master of the East Galway (1911-12) and the Staintondale (1913-14) Foxhounds. He served with the 3rd Battalion Wiltshire Regiment at St. Helena during the South African War, and rejoined his regiment, the 16th Lancers, in September, 1914. Captain Chaloner proceeded overseas in September, 1916, in command of the 20th Prisoner of War Company. He was accidentally shot by a sentry on a Prisoner of War Camp in France on the night of April 2/3, 1917, and was buried in Calais Southern Cemetery.

SECOND LIEUT. A. J. F. CHAMBERS

Warwickshire Yeomanry, T.F.

ARTHUR JOSEPH FERGUSON CHAMBERS, eldest son of James Chambers, Esquire, K.C., M.P. for South Belfast, Solicitor-General for Ireland, was born on July 25th, 1897. He was at Rugby School from 1911 to 1915, and on leaving joined the Warwickshire Yeomanry. He sailed for Egypt with a draft in April, 1916, and, after four months on the Suez Canal, his Regiment was moved to Katia, in the Sinai Peninsula. He fought against the Turks in the Battle of Bir-el-Abel, and fell while leading his men into action on the fifth day of the battle, shot through the lungs and spine, and died two days later, on August 11th, 1916. He was buried in Kantara War Memorial Cemetery, Egypt.

His commanding officer wrote:

"We are all heart-broken at the loss of "The Child", as we called him in the Regiment. He fell just as he was leading his troops into action on August 9th. His was the most charming and attractive personality, which drew everyone to him, both officers and men. As a soldier he was excellent, and, had he chosen that career, he would have gone far with it. He had all the qualities of a leader of men, the most infectious cheerfulness, steadiness in action and quick appreciation of any situation. In our memories he will never die."

And another officer wrote:

"He was my beau-ideal of a Cavalry officer."

CAPTAIN T. V. BARTLEY DENNISS

1st Royal Berkshire Regiment

THOMAS VIVIAN BARTLEY DENNISS, youngest son of Sir Edmund Bartley Denniss, Kt., M.P. for Oldham, 1911-22, was born on October 29th, 1892. He was educated at Harrow, where he was Monitor and Cadet officer in 1910, and at the Royal Military College, Sandhurst. In October, 1911, he obtained a commission direct from Sandhurst in the 1st Royal Berkshire Regiment which his great-grandfather, Lieut.-General Sir Robert Bartley, K.C.B., had commanded, and in which his great uncles had served. He was wounded at Mons in August, 1914, and again at Neuve Chapelle in March, 1915. In 1917 he commanded a battalion of his regiment with the rank of Lieut.-Colonel.

He died in hospital on August 28th, 1918, the immediate cause of death being cerebral hæmorrhage following the gunshot wound received at Neuve Chapelle, and was buried in Hillingdon Cemetery, Middlesex.

Captain Bartley Denniss was recommended three times for the D.S.O.

SECOND LIEUT. G. J. ESMONDE

26th Northumberland Fusiliers

GEOFFREY JOSEPH ESMONDE, second son of Dr. John Joseph Esmonde, M.P. for North Tipperary, 1910-15 (who himself died on service as Captain, R.A.M.C. at Tipperary Barracks on April 17th, 1915), was born on May 29th, 1897. He was educated at Clongowes Wood College, Co. Kildare, and in Germany.

He volunteered for service in 1915 and was sent to Fermoy Camp for some months, subsequently obtaining a commission in the Northumberland Fusiliers (Tyneside Irish), then under the command of his cousin, Colonel Laurence Grattan Esmonde. With them he proceeded overseas on July 12th, 1916, and after a few months' service was killed on outpost duty on October 9th, 1916. He was buried in Cité Bonjean Military Cemetery, Armentières.

His Company Commander wrote:

"His loss is genuinely felt by all with whom he came in contact. The freshness of his youth and character gave him a sincerely respected place in the Company. His coolness under fire was an inspiration to his men. He, indeed, has made the grand sacrifice and is enjoying that peace which is the battle right of heroes."

MIDSHIPMAN J. H. GRATTAN ESMONDE

Royal Navy

JOHN HENRY GRATTAN ESMONDE, second son of Sir Thomas H. Grattan Esmonde, Bart., M.P. for North Wexford, 1910-18, was born on May 8th, 1899. He was educated at Downside School, Bath, and the Royal Naval College, Osborne, and was appointed to H.M.S. *Invincible* on August 2nd, 1914. He served in the actions of Heligoland and the Falkland Islands in 1914, and also in the North Sea in 1915-16, H.M.S. *Invincible* being the Flag Ship of the 3rd Battle Cruiser Squadron. He went down with his ship at the Battle of Jutland on May 31st, 1916.

At about 6.30 p.m. on that day, *Invincible*, which had already been hit more than once by heavy shell fire without appreciable damage, was struck in "Q" turret. The shell apparently burst inside the turret. A very heavy explosion followed immediately, evidently caused by the magazine blowing up, and the ship broke in half and sank at once, only two officers and four men being subsequently picked up by the destroyer *Badger*.

His name is perpetuated on the Portsmouth Memorial.

CAPTAIN J. E. FIENNES

Gordon Highlanders

JOHN EUSTACE FIENNES was born on August 22nd, 1895. He was the only son of the Hon. Sir Eustace Fiennes, Bart., M.P. for the Banbury Division of Oxfordshire, 1906 to January, 1910, and again from December, 1910 to 1918; Governor of the Seychelles Islands from 1919 and subsequently of the Leeward Islands.

Educated first at Winton House, Winchester, he went on to Eton in September, 1909, and left in December, 1913. While at Eton he boarded at Mr. Hill's house and was fond of all games and rowing. He entered the Army from Sandhurst in 1914 and proceeded to France that year, being promoted Captain in 1915. Twice wounded in action, he was offered a Staff Course at Cambridge in 1916, but preferred to return to his regiment.

He died of wounds received in action for the third time at the capture of Infantry Hill, Arras, on June 17th, 1917, and was buried in Duisans British Cemetery.

He had a strong, thoughtful, affectionate nature and was a general favourite.

MAJOR THE REV. J. J. FITZGIBBON, S.J., M.C.

Chaplain to the Forces

JOHN JOSEPH FITZGIBBON, son of John Fitzgibbon, Esquire, M.P. for South Mayo, was born in 1882. He was educated at Clongowes Wood College, Co. Kildare, where he was prominent in games and did well at school. He subsequently spent four years in business, in which he showed great promise, and would certainly have achieved success had he not joined the Society of Jesus in 1901. The year 1907 found him back at Clongowes, and for five years he acted as Third Line and then as Lower Line Prefect. During this period as Prefect the impress of his strong personality was left on everything he took in hand, for he was essentially a man of life and action, enthusiasm and energy radiating from him. Permanent traces of his work at Clongowes live after him.

He was ordained in 1915; appointed Chaplain, 4th Class, on March 4th, 1916, embarking for France the same day, and was promoted Chaplain, 3rd Class, on January 6th, 1917. The qualities he showed as Prefect at Clongowes came out to even greater advantage in this new sphere and he was very popular with the men. Cheerful friendliness, ceaseless activity, and zeal for the men's welfare, both spiritual and temporal, were his characteristics.

He was awarded the Military Cross in March, 1918, and when the rumour went round that he had been recommended for the Victoria Cross those who knew him were not surprised. A Chaplain who knew him at the front spoke of him as "Naturally gallant and fearless."

He was killed in action on September 18th, 1918, and was buried in Trefcon British Cemetery, Caulaincourt.

CAPTAIN M. J. FITZGIBBON

Royal Dublin Fusiliers

MICHAEL JOSEPH FITZGIBBON, youngest son of John Fitzgibbon, Esquire, M.P. for South Mayo, was born on August 15th, 1886. He was educated at Clongowes Wood College, Co. Kildare, and after leaving school he studied law. He was an enthusiastic member of the Irish National Volunteers.

On the outbreak of War he went to the Curragh for training, but would not accept a commission until the Home Rule Bill had been placed on the Statute Book. He was appointed to a temporary commission as 2nd Lieutenant, Royal Dublin Fusiliers, on September 22nd, 1914, promoted Lieutenant in March, 1915, and obtained his Captaincy just before leaving for Gallipoli. He set a fine example in the attack which resulted in the capture of Chocolate Hill on the evening of August 6th, and fell while gallantly leading his Company in the fight for Kislah Dagh on August 15th, 1915, the Feast of the Assumption, and his twenty-ninth birthday.

His name is perpetuated on the Helles Memorial, Gallipoli.

A Lance-Corporal of the 5th Royal Irish Fusiliers wrote:

"When the history of this war comes before the public, that landing and taking of Suvla Bay will be mentioned, and a tribute of recognition will be paid to the two brave captains from Castlerea (Fitzgibbon and Lennon), who took the lion's share of the work in pulling their men through. Captain Fitzgibbon met with a hero's death, leading his men to victory, envied by most soldiers and regretted by all."

CAPTAIN M. A. FITZROY

4th Seaforth Highlanders

MICHAEL ALGERNON FITZROY, second son of Captain the Hon. E. A. Fitzroy, M.P. for the Daventry Division of Northamptonshire, and Speaker of the House of Commons (1928), was born on June 27th, 1895. He was educated at Rugby and Oriel College, Oxford.

When War broke out he was at Rheims, and on returning to England he joined the 4th Battalion Seaforth Highlanders, obtaining a commission as Second Lieutenant in September, 1914.

In November, 1914, he went to the front with his regiment and took part in the Battle of Neuve Chapelle, in which the Seaforth Highlanders distinguished themselves. He was slightly wounded in the shoulder, but was able to carry on. He was promoted Captain on March 11th, and was killed on April 17th, 1915, near Neuve Chapelle, while working at an advanced listening post. He was improving this post to ensure the safety of the men who occupied it, as it was exposed to enfilade and cross fire. He was buried in Cabaret-Rouge British Cemetery, Souchez.

Those who served with him and under him have borne testimony alike, not only to his popularity with all ranks, but to his ability as a leader, and power as a disciplinarian, of which his rapid promotion at so early an age furnishes an additional proof, while his high character had made a marked impression upon those who had come into contact with him during the year he had spent at Oxford.

SECOND LIEUT. J. FORSTER

2nd Battalion King's Royal Rifle Corps

JOHN FORSTER, elder son of the Rt. Hon. H. W. Forster, M.P. for the Sevenoaks Division of Kent, 1892-1919, 1st Baron Forster, Governor-General of Australia 1920-25, was born on May 13th, 1893. He went to Mr. Somerville's house at Eton in September, 1906, and entered the Army through Sandhurst, joining the 60th (K.R.R.) in 1912. He was killed at the Battle of the Marne when gallantly leading his men on September 14th, 1914. His name is perpetuated on the Memorial at La Ferté.

In a letter to his house-tutor, his father says:

"It is hard to lose Jack just as he was developing so well. I have had such wonderfully kind letters about him from some of his brother officers who were with him when he was killed, all speaking so warmly of his pluck and cheerfulness in every kind of trouble. One of his own men, who has come home wounded, told a friend of mine that they all adored him, and he did not seem to know what fear was. He had come on greatly the last two years, and I was very proud of him; but I am prouder than ever now. His battalion had got into a very awkward place, and I am told that 'he was leading his men most gallantly just at a time when they needed leading, when he was shot through the head and killed instantly.'

"I am afraid this war is going to be a long and bitter struggle, and our losses are bound to be heavy; but it does one good to think that the spirit of our fathers still lives in our sons, and that come what may we shall have the pluck to go through with it till the end."

The end could not be doubtful when the sons give their lives for a noble cause with "pluck and cheerfulness" and their fathers bear the loss in the spirit of this letter.

LIEUT. A. H. FORSTER

Royal Scots Greys

ALFRED HENRY FORSTER, younger son of the Rt. Hon. H. W. Forster, M.P. for the Sevenoaks Division of Kent, 1892-1919, 1st Baron Forster, Governor-General of Australia 1920-25, was born on February 7th, 1898. He was at Winchester from 1911-15 and went on to Sandhurst, receiving a commission in the Royal Scots Greys in July, 1916. He went to France in February, 1917, and fell seriously wounded near Le Cateau on October 17th, 1918, during the final advance. He died in hospital from the effects of these injuries on March 10th, 1919, and his ashes are deposited under the Altar in St. Catherine's Church, Exbury, Hants.

Lieut. Forster was mentioned in despatches.

CAPTAIN W. HARMOOD-BANNER

3rd South Wales Borderers

WALCOT HARMOOD-BANNER, third son of Sir John Sutherland Harmood-Banner, M.P. for the Everton Division of Liverpool, 1905-6, and since 1910, was born on August 3rd, 1882. He was educated at Winchester where he was a House Prefect and had his Football Colours. He later entered his father's business as a Chartered Accountant in Liverpool. He was an excellent shot and a keen fisherman and polo player. On the outbreak of War he joined the 3rd Battalion South Wales Borderers; he was sent to France early in 1915 and was in the continuous trench fighting of the 1st Division until his death.

In August of the same year he was promoted Captain on the field direct from Second Lieutenant, and was placed in command of a company. He was killed by a bomb while visiting posts in the trenches at Cambrin, near Béthune, on August 29th, 1915, and was buried in Cambrin Churchyard Extension.

CAPTAIN D. HENDERSON

3/8th Middlesex Regiment

DAVID HENDERSON, eldest son of the Rt. Hon. Arthur Henderson, M.P. successively since 1903 for the Barnard Castle Division of Durham, Widnes Division of Lancashire, and for Burnley, Secretary of State for Foreign Affairs, 1929, was born on December 18th, 1889. He was educated at Queen Elizabeth's Grammar School, Darlington, and was one of the assistants to Mr. John Hodge, M.P., in the office of the British Steel Smelters' Trade Union; he was also very active in the Brotherhood movement and was the youngest member of the National Council and assistant honorary secretary of the London Federation.

He joined the Public Schools Battalion of the Middlesex Regiment in September, 1914, and was later transferred to the Inns of Court O.T.C., obtaining a commission in the Middlesex Regiment in February, 1915, and his Captaincy the following June.

He applied for transfer in order to join an active service unit, proceeded overseas with the 19th London Regiment in May, 1916, and was in action at Vimy Ridge. He fell on September 16th, following, at High Wood, in the Battle of the Somme, and was buried in London Cemetery, High Wood, Longueval.

LIEUT. C. C. HENRY

2nd Worcestershire Regiment

CYRIL CHARLES HENRY, only child of Sir Charles S. Henry, Bart., M.P. for the Wellington Division of Shropshire 1906-18 and subsequently for the Wrekin Division, was born on June 28th, 1893. He was educated at Harrow.

He was stationed in Ireland at the Curragh with the 4th Hussars when War broke out, after which he was transferred to the 2nd Battalion of the Worcestershire Regiment. He proceeded to France in 1915 and fell in action on September 26th in an attack upon the Quarries, Hulluch, in the Battle of Loos.

His name is perpetuated on the Loos Memorial.

CAPTAIN G. G. HERMON-HODGE

Royal Horse Artillery

GEORGE GUY HERMON-HODGE, third son of Sir Robert Hermon-Hodge, Bart., M.P. for South Oxfordshire, 1895-1906, 1st Baron Wyfold (1919), was born on August 22nd, 1883. He was educated at Winchester and stood on Dress for Commoner XV in 1900. He passed through Woolwich, where he won "The Saddle" and played racquets against Sandhurst, and in 1903 obtained a commission in the Royal Horse Artillery. He served chiefly in Ireland before the War and made a great reputation wherever he was stationed as a sportsman and cross-country rider.

He went to France in January, 1915, in command of a Battery of Territorial Field Artillery, thence to Egypt and again back to France. He died at Doullens on July 7th, 1915, of wounds received in action on June 28th, 1915, while commanding his battery at the first Battle of the Somme, and was buried in Gézaincourt Communal Cemetery Extension.

Captain Hermon-Hodge was one of seven brothers, sons of Lord Wyfold, all serving in the War.

SECOND LIEUT. J. P. HERMON-HODGE

1st Oxford and Bucks Light Infantry

JOHN PERCIVAL HERMON-HODGE, sixth son of Sir Robert Hermon-Hodge, Bart., M.P. for South Oxfordshire, 1895-1906, 1st Baron Wyfold (1919), was born on July 18th, 1890. He was educated at Radley, where he was a Scholar, and afterwards in France. He was in business on the Cotton Exchange, Liverpool, when the War broke out and at once offered his services. He proceeded overseas with his regiment on March 29th, 1915, and was instantaneously killed on May 28th following, by a German sniper at Ploegsteert Wood, near Armentières. He was buried in Rifle House Military Cemetery, Warneton.

Second Lieut. Hermon-Hodge was the first to fall of the two of the seven sons of Lord Wyfold, serving, who lost their lives in the service of their country.

SECOND LIEUT. G. M. HEWART

6th Lincolnshire Regiment

GORDON MORLEY HEWART, eldest son of the Rt. Hon. Sir Gordon Hewart, Kt., M.P. for Leicester, 1913, until his elevation to the Peerage in 1922 as 1st Baron Hewart, Lord Chief Justice of England, was born on August 6th, 1893. He was a born student, being Head of the Classical Sixth, Manchester Grammar School, and Captain of the School.

In 1912, in the Balliol Scholarship Examination (according to the report of the examiners) his Greek Prose was not only the best, but the best paper of any kind done by anybody in the examination.

He was elected to a Domus Exhibition at Balliol College, Oxford.

In the Spring of 1914 he was placed in the First Class in Honour Classical Moderations, obtaining a First in every paper.

He then began to read Greats. As soon as the War broke out, notwithstanding defective eyesight, and continuous use of spectacles, he sought to enter the army.

He was rejected on the ground of defective sight.

A few days later, putting his spectacles in his pocket, he applied again, and was accepted.

He became a 2nd Lieutenant in the 6th (Service) Battalion, Lincolnshire Regiment.

On the 9th August, 1915, he was killed in action at Suvla Bay, a few hours after arriving, and was buried in Green Hill Cemetery, Suvla, Gallipoli.

CAPTAIN C. G. R. HIBBERT

Loyal North Lancashire Regiment

CYRIL GORDON REUSS HIBBERT, only son of Sir Henry Flemming Hibbert, Bart., M.P. for the Chorley Division of Lancashire, 1913 to 1918, was born on April 27th, 1888. He was educated at Shrewsbury, where he was a cadet, and obtained a commission on leaving school.

He was on home service from August 4th, 1914, until his regiment went to France in May, 1915, and was reported missing after the Battle of Festubert, on June 15th, 1915. His body was never recovered, but his name is perpetuated on the Le Touret Memorial.

LIEUT. W. P. HINDS

15th London Welsh Fusiliers

WILLIAM PUGH HINDS, only son of John Hinds, Esquire, M.P. for West Carmarthenshire, was born on May 10th, 1897. He was educated at Christ's College, Blackheath, and Bishop's Stortford College. He was engaged in engineering at the Electrical Standardizing, Testing, and Training Institution, Faraday House, when the War broke out, joining his battalion in September, 1914, and proceeding overseas in December, 1915. He died on February 2nd, 1916, from wounds received in action, and was buried in Merville Communal Cemetery.

SECOND LIEUT. I. G. JOHN

South Wales Borderers

IORWERTH GLYNDWR JOHN, third son of Edward T. John, Esquire, M.P. for East Denbighshire 1910-18, was born on October 21st, 1894. He was educated at New College, Harrogate, and Balliol College, Oxford. After training with the Oxford O.T.C. he was gazetted on April 12th, 1915, joining the Special Reserve of Officers and becoming attached to the South Wales Borderers. He left for France on October 1st, 1915, returned to this country in January, and left for France again on January 17th, 1916. He fell in action at the Battle of Loos, on February 25th, 1916, and was buried in St. Mary's A.D.S. Cemetery, Haisnes. His Colonel wrote:

"The line of trench which we have just left, where he was killed, was a very nasty one, with two large mine craters just in front of it. The enemy was very active in these craters and we had had some pretty severe fighting to maintain ourselves on our edge of them. Your son was on duty in the front line just below one of the craters, when he was struck by a trench mortar and killed instantly. We all very much mourn his loss. He was such a clever boy, and always so willing to do anything that was wanted, that his death is a serious loss to the regiment."

In his death Wales lost an ardent young Nationalist who, had he been spared, might have played a significant part in public life. Passionately fond of Welsh music, a keen Eisteddfodwr, he was at one time Secretary, and later Treasurer, of the Cambrian Society at Oxford. While at Oxford, he became a member of the Fabian Society, leaning to its outlook on social questions.

CAPTAIN J. K. LAW

7th Royal Fusiliers and Royal Flying Corps

JAMES KIDSTON LAW, eldest son of the Rt. Hon. Andrew Bonar Law, M.P. for the Central Division of Glasgow, and Prime Minister, 1922, was born on September 20th, 1893. He was educated at a private school, Heddon Court, New Barnet, and went on to Marlborough College, which he represented at hockey and football. From Marlborough he went direct into the City and until the outbreak of War served with the "Royal Securities Corporation," which firm he left on securing a commission in the 7th Royal Fusiliers in August, 1914. After spending some months training at Falmouth he proceeded to France in March, 1916, and after having been wounded in June transferred to the Royal Flying Corps. Having served in this country as an instructor for some time, he returned in September, 1917, to France with 60 Squadron.

The following is taken from the "History of 60 Squadron R.A.F." by Group-Capt. A. J. L. Scott:

"—It was in September, 1917, that Capt. J. K. Law joined at Marle Capelle. He was a tiger to fight, and had he come through his first month would probably have made a great name for himself. He did several shows over the line and his machine was badly shot about in every one of them. On September 21st a patrol operating in the neighbourhood of Roulers saw 24 hostile machines and engaged 8 of them. A general engagement took place in the course of which Law was shot down and killed."

His name is perpetuated on the Arras Memorial.

LIEUT. C. J. LAW
3rd K.O.S.B.

CHARLES JOHN LAW, second son of the Rt. Hon. Andrew Bonar Law, M.P. for the Central Division of Glasgow and Prime Minister, 1922, was born at Helensburgh on 21st February, 1897. He was educated at Heddon Court, New Barnet; he went on to Eton in 1911, and on leaving Eton went to Weimar to study German. He arrived back in England on August 3rd, 1914, by the last train out of Germany before War was declared and in the same month received his commission in the K.O.S.B. He did his training at Edinburgh but in 1915 was so seriously ill with rheumatic fever that he was unable to go to France with his battalion, and finally proceeded to Egypt in October, 1916, with the 5th Battalion. He fell in action at the second Battle of Gaza on April 19th, 1917, and was buried in Gaza War Cemetery, Palestine.

LIEUT. HUGH LOGAN

Leicestershire Yeomanry

HUGH LOGAN, second son of John W. Logan, Esquire, M.P. for the Harborough Division of Leicestershire, 1891 to 1904, and 1910 to 1916, was born on May 10th, 1885. He was educated at Westminster School, where he was Captain of the Cricket XI, and at Trinity Hall, Cambridge. He was a partner in the firm of Logan and Hemingway, Railway Contractors, up to the time of joining the Army. He went overseas in October, 1918, and died of pneumonia at Tournai, in Belgium, while attached to the Royal Engineers, and was buried in the Communal Cemetery there.

BRIGADIER-GENERAL W. LONG, C.M.G., D.S.O.

Commanding 56th Brigade, 19th Division

WALTER LONG, eldest son of the Right Hon. Walter H. Long, M.P., First Lord of the Admiralty, 1919 to 1921; 1st Viscount Long (1921), was born on July 26th, 1879. He was educated at Harrow School and was Champion Light Weight Boxer, and twice won the Middle Weight Boxing Championship of the British Army.

Brigadier-General Long was gazetted to the Scots Greys in 1899. He served through the South African War and was wounded at Dronberg, after the Relief of Kimberley, having taken part in the famous ride of Sir John French. He was twice mentioned in despatches and received the D.S.O. Part of the time he served as A.D.C. to General Bruce Hamilton.

He went to France in August, 1914, being then Captain in charge of a Squadron, and was shortly afterwards promoted Major, then Lieut.-Colonel Commanding the 6th Battalion, Wiltshire Regiment, and received the C.M.G.; he also had the Order of St. Stanislas, 2nd class with swords. He was several times mentioned in despatches, and promoted to Brigadier-General Commanding 56th Brigade, 19th Division, and made a Brevet Lieut.-Colonel.

He was killed in action when in the trenches at Hébuterne on January 28th, 1917, and was buried in Couin British Cemetery.

His Majesty the King wrote:

"The Queen and I are deeply grieved to hear that your son has been killed in action after such a distinguished career, and in the prime of youth. I regret that my Army has lost one of its promising young Generals."

H.R.H. the Duke of Connaught wrote:

"In Toby the Army and the Scots Greys have lost a splendid Officer, who has always set the finest example and whose name will long be remembered. His has been a glorious death, falling in action in command of his Brigade."

Field-Marshal Sir Douglas Haig wrote:

"As the General under whom he was directly serving will have told you, his death deprives the Army of one of our best Brigadiers. As a soldier he was so practical, and thoroughly up to his work. I always felt he was sure to attain high rank, and, as a man, he was loved and admired by us for his manly straightforward ways."

LIEUT. G. A. LOYD

2nd Scots Guards

GEOFFREY ARCHIBALD LOYD, third son of Archie Kirkman Loyd, Esquire, K.C., M.P. for the Abingdon Division of Berkshire, 1895-1905 and 1916-1918, was born on January 22nd, 1890. He was educated at Eton and Magdalen College, Oxford, and as a sportsman was fond of rowing and fox-hunting. He was gazetted 2nd Lieutenant in the Scots Guards in February, 1913, and promoted Lieutenant on September 24th, 1914. He embarked with the Expeditionary Force on August 12th, 1914, and was present at engagements at Mons, Landrecies, on the Aisne, and at Ypres. He was attached, with a cyclist company, to the Mounted Troops of the 2nd Division, and, in recognition of his services during the rearguard actions in the retirement from Mons, was awarded the Legion of Honour and was also mentioned in Sir John French's despatch of January 31st, 1915.

He fell in action at Zonnebeke, near Ypres, on November 13th, 1914, while engaged with his cyclist company in holding on to an entrenched position as escort to howitzer guns which were being fiercely shelled by the enemy. He was buried in Poperinghe Communal Cemetery.

LIEUT. D. C. D. MACMASTER

6th Queen's Own Cameron Highlanders

DONALD CAMERON DEFORD MACMASTER, only son of Sir Donald Macmaster, Bart., M.P. for the Chertsey Division of Surrey, 1910-1918, was born on September 4th, 1894, in Montreal, Canada.

He was at Rugby from 1908 to 1911, and, after a year spent in study, at Tours, in France, he then entered Trinity College, Cambridge. He was still an undergraduate, and following the Law Courses at Lincoln's Inn, when gazetted to the Cameron Highlanders in August, 1914. He went to the front with his battalion in July, 1915.

His battalion formed part of the gallant 15th (Highland) Division in the great advance on Loos and Lens on September 25th, 1915, on which day he fell "gallantly leading his men," says the official report, "just in front of the first line of German trenches." He was buried in Dud Corner Cemetery, Loos.

All his senior officers were killed in the same action, but a corporal of his company who was with him when he fell wrote:

"His Platoon would have followed him anywhere, as they had the greatest faith in him as a leader. They say and feel he will never be replaced."

SECOND LIEUT. G. T. G. McMICKING

Cambridgeshire Regiment, T.F.

GILBERT THOMAS GORE McMICKING, eldest son of Major McMicking, C.M.G., M.P. for Kirkcudbrightshire, 1906-10, and 1910-18, was born on August 2nd, 1894. He was educated at Marlborough and trained with the O.T.C., then passed on to Trinity College, Cambridge, and, whilst at the University, received a commission in the Cambridgeshire Regiment. He was reading for a degree in Modern Languages and at the beginning of the Long Vacation in 1914 went to Weimar to study German literature under Professor Francke. Hearing rumours of war, he wrote to the Adjutant of his regiment for information, but his letters were opened by the German authorities and, upon the declaration of War, he was immediately seized by the police at Weimar. He was kept in solitary confinement in the military cells at Weimar for six weeks and then, as a belligerent, was transferred to the Castle of Celle. He escaped during the winter of 1916-17, but, after three days and nights of exposure to severe weather, he was so incapacitated by illness and hunger that he had to give himself up. Later, he was interned in Holland, as a prisoner of war and died at Bois-le-Duc, on Armistice Day, November 11th, 1918, from acute influenza, his constitution having been undermined by the privations he had suffered during three and a half years' captivity in Germany. He was buried in Orthen Protestant Cemetery, Holland.

CAPTAIN G. C. N. NICHOLSON

Royal Flying Corps

GEORGE CROSFIELD NORRIS NICHOLSON, only son of Sir Charles Nicholson, Bart., M.P. for Doncaster, was born on November 19th, 1884. He was educated at Eton and Clare College, Cambridge. In 1910 he was assistant private secretary to the Rt. Hon. Edmund Robertson, Parliamentary Secretary to the Admiralty, and in the following year went to the War Office as private secretary to Colonel the Rt. Hon. J. E. B. Seely, then Under Secretary for War, to whom he later became principal private secretary when Secretary of State for War, 1912-1914.

He was killed on March 11th, 1916, when flying in England, and was buried in Hurley Churchyard, Berkshire.

Captain Nicholson took up flying at the outbreak of War and rapidly became a proficient pilot. His death was a serious loss not only to the Royal Flying Corps, but to the whole future of flying in England; he was regarded as one of the men who would have done most after the war to develop the new service.

LIEUT. W. H. E. NIELD

11th Royal Fusiliers

WILFRED HERBERT EVERARD NIELD, elder son of the Rt. Hon. Sir Herbert Nield, K.C., M.P. for the Ealing Division of Middlesex, 1906-18, and since continuously for the Borough of Ealing, was born on February 16th, 1891. He was educated at Winchester, where he was a House Prefect and showed promise as a long-distance runner, and at Merton College, Oxford. Here he played a leading part in the life of the College and commanded the Merton contingent of the O.T.C. On leaving Oxford he went to Weimar to acquire German, and subsequently to France in order to prepare for the entrance examination for the Diplomatic Service. He was in France when War was declared, but returned to England as soon as he was allowed to do so and obtained a commission in September, 1914. He returned to France with his regiment in July, 1915, and was wounded at an advanced post near Fricourt in December. While in England recovering from wounds, he took his degree at Oxford, rejoining his battalion at the front in May, 1916. On July 1st, 1916, the opening day of the British attack in the Valley of the Somme, his company was selected to occupy the front line trenches, and as soon as the barrage was lifted, he led his men over the top in the first wave of the advance towards Montauban. After proceeding some distance he was struck by a shot which completely severed his left wrist, but, refusing to go back to the dressing station, continued to advance until another shot struck him in the leg and made further progress impossible. He was then placed with others in a deep shell hole near by, when a few moments later a shell burst in the hole and killed all its occupants.

Lieut. Nield, due for his Captaincy when he fell, was buried on the battlefield; in May, 1919, his body was removed to the Dantzig Alley Cemetery, on the highway from Mametz to Montauban.

A fearless fidelity to the claims of honour, of brotherhood and of duty seemed to come naturally and instinctively to Wilfred Nield. Those qualities, which at first endeared him to his friends at school and college and later to those who served with and under him, showed him to be going from strength to strength as his character broadened and developed with each fresh experience during his short life. It was these same qualities which prompted his soldier-servant to write of him that he was "an officer and a gentleman in the true sense of the word—and a good pal in a tight corner."

His Commanding Officer wrote:

"The men of his Platoon had complete confidence in him, and the gallant way in which he led them is beyond any praise my words can express. I cannot say how much I deplore his loss, for I too, had the utmost confidence in him. I never had a finer officer."

LIEUT. H. N. NUTTALL

Royal Army Service Corps

HARRY NORBURY NUTTALL, elder son of Harry Nuttall, Esquire, M.P. for the Stretford Division of Lancashire, 1906-1918, was born on May 31st, 1887. He was educated at Harrow and Lincoln College, Oxford, where he took Honours in Law. He was engaged in business as an India and China merchant in Manchester and joined the Army Service Corps in 1915.

Lieut. Nuttall proceeded to France in 1916, and died of wounds received in action on July 14th, 1917. He was buried in Lijssenthoek Military Cemetery, Poperinghe.

SECOND LIEUT. W. J. O'MALLEY

Royal Field Artillery

WILLIAM JOSEPH O'MALLEY, only son of William O'Malley, M.P. for the Connemara Division of Co. Galway, 1895-1918, was born on November 30th, 1891. He was educated at St. Augustine's College, Ramsgate, where he took first place in mathematics and science and was proficient in games. He was articled to Sir W. B. Peat and Company, Chartered Accountants when war broke out, and joined the 6th London Brigade, Royal Field Artillery, in September, 1914. He proceeded overseas on October 9th, 1915; was killed in action near Ypres on April 9th, 1917, and was buried at Bedford House Cemetery, Zillebeke.

LIEUT. W. P. ORDE-POWLETT

1/4th Yorkshire Regiment

WILLIAM PERCY ORDE-POWLETT, eldest son of the Hon. Algar Orde-Powlett, M.P. for the Richmond Division of Yorkshire, 1910-1918, was born in April, 1894.

He was educated at Eton and Cambridge.

The news of his death at the early age of twenty, just a month after he started for the front, came as a shock to many friends. He had been through two terrible fights near Ypres without a wound, but, as he stood up in the trenches on the morning of May 17th, 1915, was shot in the neck by a sniper and died immediately. He spent five happy years at Eton and distinguished himself in Science, Botany being his special subject. There can be little doubt he would have gained high honours at Cambridge in the Natural Science Tripos. He was a very close and painstaking observer and would work long hours at the microscope with real pleasure. Science has lost an able and enthusiastic worker who would have made a name for himself in days to come. He was a member of the Boats, also of the E.C.O.T.C. and enjoyed a healthy, outdoor life. Always a great reader and a serious-minded boy, he had shrewd common sense and a refreshing humour. He happily combined uprightness, gentleness and high principle.

His name is perpetuated on the Menin Gate Memorial, Ypres.

SECOND LIEUT. G. V. PEARCE

2nd Royal Warwickshire Regiment

GEOFFREY VINCENT PEARCE, only son of Sir William Pearce, Kt., M.P. for Tower Hamlets, 1906-1918, and for Limehouse, 1918-1922, was born on June 19th, 1889. He was educated at Uppingham School and in Germany, and was a good football player and runner. He subsequently entered his father's business of Chemical Manufacturer in East London.

He afterwards joined the Artists' Rifles and was one of their team for bayonet fighting, etc., at the Royal Military Tournament, 1914; he embarked with them for France in September. In October, 1914, when the Artists' Rifles had become an Officers Training Corps, he was in the first fifty selected for commissions and received his in the 2nd Battalion Royal Warwickshire Regiment.

He fell in action on December 18th, 1914, at Rouge Bancs, near Armentières, while leading his men in an attack on the German trenches, and his name is perpetuated on the Ploegsteert Memorial.

His Company Commander wrote that in him the battalion lost a very promising officer, and one who was universally popular with all ranks.

LIEUT. R. H. PIKE PEASE

1st Coldstream Guards

RONALD HERBERT PIKE PEASE, elder son of the Rt. Hon. Herbert Pike Pease, M.P. for Darlington from 1898 until his elevation to the Peerage in 1923 as 1st Baron Daryngton, was born on October 3rd, 1896. Educated at Eton, he took Fifth Form from Stone House in 1910 and left in December, 1914, to take a commission in the Coldstream Guards.

In those four years he always did the day's work in the day and did it well, and his future career seemed bright with promise.

His face, full of light and intelligence, thoughtfulness, kindly humour and good sense, was a true reflection of his mind and character. He had a large measure of success at Eton; he was Captain of his House, a member of "Pop," and got his "XXII" before he was 18; but success only served to bring out his sterling qualities, and he offered himself to his country at the earliest moment in the hour of her need. His death leaves "the quiet sense of something lost," but yet with an undying memory, beyond words, of a fair young life well lived and freely given for a great cause.

He fell in action at Ginchy, in the Battle of the Somme, on September 15th, 1916, and with him something particularly bright and wholesome went out of life. He was buried in the Guards Cemetery, Lesbœufs.

His Commanding Officer, Lieut.-Col. the Hon. G. V. Baring, M.P., commemorated elsewhere in this volume, was killed on the same day, an occasion, unique in the history of the Coldstream Guards, afforded by the Battle of the Somme as that on which all three battalions of the regiment attacked in line together.

LIEUT. T. WHITAKER POLLARD

10th Lancashire Fusiliers

THOMAS WHITAKER POLLARD, second son of Sir George Pollard, M.P. for the Eccles Division of Lancashire, 1906-18, was born on December 27th, 1890. He was educated at Marlborough College, where he was in the Football XV in 1908, and twice won the heavy weight boxing. On leaving Marlborough he studied Law. He joined the Army in August, 1914, and was posted to the 10th Lancashire Fusiliers. He went to France in 1915 and was invalided home after twelve months in the Ypres Salient.

In 1917 he rejoined his regiment in France and fell in action at Gavrelle, near Arras, on May 16th, 1917. His name is perpetuated on the Arras Memorial.

CAPTAIN C. T. A. POLLOCK

1/4th East Yorkshire Regiment

CHARLES THOMAS ANDERDON POLLOCK, only son of Sir Ernest M. Pollock, K.C., K.B.E., M.P. for Warwick and Leamington, 1910-23, Master of the Rolls (1923) and 1st Baron Hanworth (Cr. 1926), was born on April 12th, 1889. Whilst most boys of his age were attending their preparatory schools, he was travelling round the world by way of Australia and California, where he stayed some months for the benefit of his health. He went to Wellington College in the summer of 1903, his uncle, the present Bishop of Norwich, being then Headmaster. His short stay at Wellington did not enable him to figure prominently in games or work and at the age of 17 he went up to Trinity College, Cambridge, with a view to trying for a University Commission.

At Trinity, which for generations had been a stronghold of his family, he gained second class honours in Part I and II of the Historical Tripos. He was a member of the College Hockey XI and was a frequent speaker at the various College Debating Societies.

His plans for the Army were changed when an old friend of his father's offered to take him into his office, and in 1909 he joined the firm of Messrs. Thomson, Hankey & Co., of Mincing Lane, E.C., with whom he stayed till the outbreak of War.

He had served in the Rifle Corps at Wellington and Cambridge and when he began working in London he joined the Inns of Court O.T.C.

On the outbreak of War, he was at once given a commission and spent three years training officers in England and France. In spite of his repeated efforts, it was not till 1917 that he was allowed to transfer to a combatant unit. He was attached to the 1/4th East Yorkshire Regiment and served with this unit during the operations at Passchendaele and in the retreat of March, 1918.

It was on March 31st (Easter Day), 1918, when retiring with his battalion, which he was temporarily commanding, that his batman, who was wounded and likely to fall into the hands of the enemy, called out to him for help. Captain Pollock at once ran back to him and tried to carry him on his back to a place of safety. Unfortunately, this gallant self-sacrifice was in vain as he was shot through the heart and his batman was taken prisoner. He fell at Demouin, near Villers-Bretonneaux, and was buried in Moreuil Communal Cemetery.

It was not till several months later, when the batman was released by the Germans, that the story of Captain Pollock's gallantry was made known.

He had a most attractive personality. His wit, charm and sincerity endeared him to all. At Wellington and Trinity many sought his companionship and deemed it a privilege to be numbered amongst his friends. Possibly his travels when still a child had widened his mind to an exceptional degree, for whilst he had the clearest views upon what was right and wrong, there was nothing narrow in his judgment of his friends and contemporaries.

Captain Pollock was twice mentioned in despatches.

LIEUT. R. J. PROTHERO

7th Hussars

ROWLAND JOHN PROTHERO, only son of the Rt. Hon. Rowland E. Prothero, President of the Board of Agriculture and Fisheries, 1916-19, M.P. for the University of Oxford from 1914 until his elevation to the Peerage as 1st Baron Ernle in 1919, was born on June 3rd, 1894. He was educated at Eton and his sturdy figure will not be forgotten, nor his endurance at football, in which he captained Mr. Vaughan's House in 1911

A lover of open-air life and of horses, he chose the Army for his profession, and a cavalry regiment; and after passing through Sandhurst, went out to join the 7th Hussars in India. From India he went with them in 1917 to Mesopotamia, and, after taking part in much fighting, died at Jift on November 8th, 1918, from wounds received at the crossing of the Lesser Zab. He was buried in Baghdad War Cemetery.

"His pluck," wrote his Commanding Officer, "was exceptional; the way in which the other officers received my news of his death, said volumes for his character." "He was always in front," writes another fellow-officer, "whether after a fox or pig in peace, or when he was with his men in war."

Courage and modesty: these are characteristics of an English gentleman, and they were well exemplified in his career.

SUB-LIEUT. J. F. ROYDS

Royal Navy

JASPER FRANCIS ROYDS, second son of Colonel Royds, M.P. for the Sleaford Division of Lincolnshire, 1910-22, was born on October 19th, 1896. He was educated at Eton, and, entering the Navy, was appointed to H.M.S. *Commonwealth* in 1915, becoming sub-lieutenant in April, 1917. He had command of a Picquet boat in action at Zeebrugge in 1917, and was killed on November 9th in that year through accidental collision with a R.N.A.S. lorry while riding a motor bicycle. He was buried in Fulbeck Churchyard, Lincolnshire.

SECOND LIEUT. T. W. RUSSELL

10th Royal Dublin Fusiliers

THOMAS WALLACE RUSSELL, only son of the Rt. Hon. Sir T. W. Russell, Bart., M.P. for South Tyrone 1886-1910, and for North Tyrone 1911-18, was born on May 18th, 1897. He was educated at Trinity College, Dublin, and received his commission on November 13th, 1915. He proceeded to France with his battalion in August, 1916, and was killed in action at Beaumont Hamel on November 13th, exactly one year from the date of receiving his commission.

He was buried in Knightsbridge Cemetery, Mesnil-Martinsart.

SECOND LIEUT. J. H. CLAVELL SALTER

1/5th King's Own Royal Lancashire Regiment

JOHN HENRY CLAVELL SALTER, only son of the Hon. Mr. Justice Salter, M.P. for the Basingstoke Division of Hampshire, 1906-17, was born in August, 1899. He was educated at Wellington, where he was in the Stanley from 1912 to 1916, and at Sandhurst. He received his commission in the Regular Army at the age of 19, and went overseas immediately. He was killed near Le Touret on April 9th, 1918, while helping to stem the great German attack in which the 55th Division so nobly sacrificed itself.

Though only nineteen years of age at the time of his death, he took with him a fine record from his school and his regiment. His name is perpetuated on the Loos Memorial.

CAPTAIN A. P. I. SAMUELS

11th Royal Irish Rifles

ARTHUR PUREFOY IRWIN SAMUELS, only son of the Hon. Mr. Justice Samuels, M.P. for Dublin University, 1917-19, was born on February 14th, 1887. He was educated at St. Stephen's School, Dublin, and Dublin University, taking his M.A. degree with First Honours; Gold Medallist and Senior Moderator in History and Political Science, and Auditor of the College Historical Society, 1910-11. He became a lieutenant in the Dublin University O.T.C. in June, 1914, joining up on the outbreak of War and receiving his Captaincy in the Royal Irish Rifles (Ulster Division) on February 1st, 1915. He went overseas with the 36th Ulster Division on October 4th, 1915, serving in the trenches on the Ancre and the Somme and at Thiepval Wood, 1915-16. He was wounded at the commencement of the Battle of the Somme, and later served in the Ypres Salient. He fell in action opposite Messines at midnight on September 24th, 1916, and was buried in Ration Farm (La Plus Douve) Annexe, Ploegsteert.

CAPTAIN C. G. SEELY

1/8th Hampshire Regiment (Isle of Wight Rifles)

CHARLES GRANT SEELY, eldest son of Sir Charles Seely, Bart., M.P. for the Mansfield Division of Notts, 1916-18, was born on November 29th, 1894, and was educated at Eton. He was at Trinity College, Cambridge, when the War broke out. He enlisted on August 4th, 1914, in the Hampshire Regiment, and received a commission in the regiment a few days later. He served in the Isle of Wight during the winter, and was promoted lieutenant in April, 1915. He accompanied the regiment to Gallipoli, landing there on August 10th, 1915. After the action at Suvla Bay on August 13th he became temporary captain and acting adjutant, which post he held till they left the peninsula in December, 1915, for another front. He served on outposts in command of a company during the summer and autumn of 1916, and was promoted captain in July, 1916. He was present during much fighting, and was killed in command of his company close to the enemy position, after being wounded three times during the advance, at Tank Redoubt, Gaza, on April 19th, 1917. He was buried in Gaza War Cemetery, Palestine.

His lovable nature was well expressed in the words of his Colonel:

"On or off duty he had endeared himself to his company to a degree which might fairly be called worship." And he writes of his final advance, "There were two battalions in line in front of us, the advance was very rapid in the face of heavy shelling and machine-gun fire. The third and fourth lines progressed so well that they actually passed through the leading battalion and were first in the enemy trenches. Soon after the start it was reported to me that he was wounded in the foot, but had not stopped and was still leading his company, and half an hour later it was reported that he was knocked over. It is hardly necessary for me to say how much we miss him —officers and men, Brigade and Division."

Another writer said:

"I was so sorry to hear about young Seely, he was such a splendid boy. He was beloved by his men and by everyone who knew him."

Captain Seely was mentioned in despatches.

LIEUT. F. R. SEELY

1st Hampshire Regiment

FRANK REGINALD SEELY, eldest son of Major-General the Rt. Hon. J. E. B. Seely, C.B., C.M.G., D.S.O., M.P. for the Ilkeston Division of Derbyshire, 1910-14; Secretary of State for War, 1911-12-14, was born on June 26th, 1896. He was educated at Harrow, going on to Sandhurst from the Upper Sixth, in February, 1915, and in the following August was gazetted to the Hampshire Regiment. He was appointed A.D.C. to his father when in command of the Canadian Cavalry Brigade and joined that unit in France in March, 1916.

He fell in action at the Battle of Arras on April 13th, 1917, and was buried in Haute-Avesnes British Cemetery.

SECOND LIEUT. D. J. SHEEHAN

Royal Flying Corps

DANIEL JOSEPH SHEEHAN, eldest son of Captain Sheehan, M.P. for Mid-Cork, 1901-6 and 1907-18, was born on November 14th, 1894. He was educated at Christian College, Cork, and Mount St. Joseph's College, Roscrea. He played for Munster two years in the Senior Colleges Inter-Provincial Rugby Championships and was considered the best three-quarter back in Ireland. He joined Devitt and Moore's Ocean Training Ship *Medway* as a cadet in 1912, winning subsequently first prize for Navigation and General Seamanship. He transferred to H.M.S. *Hibernia* as midshipman, R.N.R., for training with a view to a permanent commission in the Navy. After serving with the 3rd Battle Squadron in the North Sea, in 1914-15, he was transferred to the Naval Air Service, obtaining his aviator's certificate in 1915. He was wounded while flying in Belgium, and, being regarded as unfit for further service with the Naval Air Force, received permission to transfer to the Royal Flying Corps. He was engaged for a time as Instructor at Oxford, then went on active service again. He met his death on May 10th, 1917, when, on a scouting expedition, a superior body of enemy aircraft engaged the British battle-plane, and Lieut. Sheehan and another officer were killed. He was buried in Cabaret-Rouge British Cemetery, Souchez.

His superior officer wrote:

"He was loved by all and was by nature absolutely devoid of fear."

SECOND LIEUT. M. J. SHEEHAN

Royal Flying Corps

MARTIN JOSEPH SHEEHAN, second son of Captain Sheehan, M.P. for Mid-Cork, 1901-6 and 1907-18, was born in March, 1896. He was educated at Christian College, Cork, and Mount St. Joseph's College, Roscrea. He won several prizes in school sports and played for Munster in the Rugby Inter-Provincial Senior College Championships, being described in the Dublin Press as "the most brilliant three-quarter back the College had produced for years." He went to Canada in 1913, and was employed in the Union Bank of Canada at Bassano and Bellevue, Alberta. He joined the Canadian Expeditionary Force as a private in 1915 and won the all-round Athletic Championship of his Division in Nova Scotia. He came overseas with his battalion in 1916, and transferred as a cadet to the Royal Munster Fusiliers, and later obtained his commission. With them he was in some of the fiercest fighting at Passchendaele and elsewhere. He transferred to the Royal Air Service as "Observer" and saw considerable service in France and Italy with the 13th Squadron.

He went out on observation duty over the enemy lines on the morning of October 1st, 1918, and met his death, but in what circumstances has never been known. He was buried in Anneux British Cemetery.

LIEUT. W. E. D. SHORTT

1st Scots Guards

WILLIAM EDWARD DUDLEY SHORTT, only son of the Rt. Hon. Edward Shortt, K.C., M.P. for Newcastle-upon-Tyne, West, 1910-22; Home Secretary, 1919-22, was born on October 23rd, 1892. He was educated at Charterhouse, where he was in the Cricket XI. He passed into Sandhurst, but was rejected for the Army on account of his eyesight and was with the firm of Furness, Withy and Company until the outbreak of War. He at once enlisted in the 115th Battalion East Surrey Regiment and, after a period of two months' service at home, proceeded with his Unit to Cawnpore where he served from December 4th, 1914, until August 20th, 1915. He subsequently proceeded with his battalion to Nowshera, North-West Frontier, and remained there until October, when he returned to England—sent back by his Colonel specially to get a commission.

On December 4th, 1915, he was given a commission as Second Lieutenant in the Special Reserve of Officers, Scots Guards, and proceeded to France for service with the 1st Battalion Scots Guards in the Guards Division on April 1st, 1916. Whilst serving in France he was promoted Lieutenant on July 19th, 1916. He fell in action on October 12th, 1917, and was buried in Bleuet Farm British Cemetery, Elverdinghe.

His Colonel wrote:

"Dudley was loved by everyone in the Battalion, officers and men, and he indeed can ill be spared. He was absolutely fearless and a splendid officer."

LIEUT. J. F. SMALLWOOD, M.C.

11th Middlesex Regiment

JAMES FENEMORE SMALLWOOD, eldest son of Edward Smallwood, Esquire, M.P. for East Islington, 1917-18, was born on December 8th, 1891. He was educated privately. He joined up in September, 1914, and obtained a commission in the 14th Middlesex Regiment in December following. A year later he was transferred to the 11th Middlesex Regiment and proceeded overseas with it, being present at the Battle of the Somme in 1916, and at the first Battle of Arras in 1917. He died of wounds received in action at Monchy-le-Preux on May 22nd, 1917, and was buried in Etaples Military Cemetery.

Lieut. Smallwood was mentioned in despatches and awarded the Military Cross.

CAPTAIN E. B. SMALLWOOD, M.C.

1st Hertfordshire Regiment

ERIC BUTLER SMALLWOOD, second son of Edward Smallwood, Esquire, M.P. for East Islington, 1917-18, was born on January 8th, 1895. He was educated privately. He joined up in November, 1914, and trained with the Inns of Court O.T.C. receiving subsequently a commission in the 1st Hertfordshire Regiment. Proceeding overseas in September, 1915, he took part in the Battle of Loos, the first Battle of the Somme, and of the Ancre. He fell in action at Ypres on January 7th, 1917, while superintending measures for the safety of his men, and was buried in Essex Farm Cemetery, Boesinghe.

Captain Smallwood was awarded the Military Cross.

MAJOR G. H. SOAMES

1st West Yorkshire Regiment

GILBERT HORSMAN SOAMES, second son of Arthur Wellesley Soames, Esquire, M.P. for South Norfolk 1898-1918, was born on April 8th, 1879. He was educated at Charterhouse and privately, and studied medicine. In April, 1900, he obtained a commission in the Lancashire Fusiliers and served in the South African War, receiving the Queen's Medal with 3 clasps and the King's Medal with 2 clasps. Later, he transferred to the West Yorkshire Regiment. In 1914 he was Adjutant of the 5th South Staffordshire Regiment and went to France with that Unit in February 1915. After being invalided home, he rejoined his old Regiment, the 1st West Yorkshires, in France, acting as Lieut.-Colonel. He was shot by a sniper at night in "No Man's Land" near La Bassée on January 9th, 1917, and was buried in Cambrin Churchyard.

Major Soames was mentioned in despatches.

MAJOR M. G. SOAMES

Royal Horse Artillery

MAURICE GORDON SOAMES, youngest son of Arthur Wellesley Soames, Esquire, M.P. for South Norfolk, 1898-1918, was born on February 3rd, 1884. He was educated at Eton, and won a scholarship at Wellington, but did not take it up. He passed direct from Eton into Woolwich and out into the Royal Field Artillery, serving in Ireland and in various places at home. He later joined the Royal Horse Artillery in India and was at home on leave when War was declared. In September, 1914, he was sent out to "J" Battery, R.H.A., on the Aisne, and subsequently took part in both battles of Ypres and in the battle of the Somme. He died at a casualty clearing station on September 24th, 1916, of multiple wounds received the previous day while in command of "A" Battery, 48th Division, on the Somme.

The adjutant of his brigade wrote that the Divisional Artillery had lost rather heavily, but that his was far the heaviest loss they had sustained. "We all loved him."

Major Soames was buried in Heilly Station Cemetery, Méricourt-l'Abbé.

LIEUT. C. STANTON

10th Welch Regiment

CLIFFORD STANTON, elder son of Charles Butt Stanton, Esquire, C.B.E., J.P., M.P. for Merthyr Tydfil, 1915, was born on April 23rd, 1894. He was educated at Intermediate and Higher Grade Schools and was a Silver and Gold Medallist for proficiency on the violin.

He joined up in August, 1914, and went overseas early in 1915, taking part in engagements at Mametz Wood, Irish Farm, and in the Ypres salient. He captured a flag from the German trenches single-handed and for this exploit received special mention.

He fell in action at Pilkem on the first day of the third Battle of Ypres, July 31st, 1917, on the occasion on which the British and French attacked on a 15 mile front taking 12 villages and 5,000 prisoners. He was buried in No Man's Cot British Cemetery, Boesinghe.

Lieut. Stanton was mentioned in despatches.

LIEUT. V. A. STRAUSS

Royal Flying Corps

VICTOR ARTHUR STRAUSS, elder son of Arthur Strauss, Esquire, M.P. for North Paddington, 1910-18, was born on September 22nd, 1894. He was educated at Rugby and, after going to France and Germany to learn the languages, he entered his father's business in London. In January, 1915, he joined the Inns of Court O.T.C., and, receiving his commission in the Army Service Corps in May, he went to the front in France in October. In the summer of 1916, he was attached to the Royal Flying Corps as an Observer, and was killed during an air flight at the Battle of the Somme on November 27th, 1916. His name is perpetuated on the Arras Memorial.

His Commanding Officer in the Army Service Corps wrote:

"Many friends of mine have been killed, but I have felt his death ten times more than any one else's. I had the greatest admiration for him."

SECOND LIEUT. H. TENNANT

Royal Scots Greys (attached Royal Flying Corps)

HENRY TENNANT, eldest son of the Rt. Hon. Harold John Tennant, M.P. for Berwickshire, 1894-1918, Under Secretary of State for War, 1912-16, was born on June 9th, 1897. He was educated at Eton and Sandhurst, where he spent three months in the Cavalry Company. He received a commission in the 2nd Dragoons (Royal Scots Greys) in November, 1915, but was immediately attached to the R.F.C. and went through his preliminary instruction at Farnborough. On leaving Farnborough he was sent to Croydon, where he met with a very serious accident while flying on May 27th, 1916, which nearly cost him his life. On recovering from the effects of this, he rejoined for service with the R.F.C. and was sent to Wye, where he acted for a short time as Instructor. On April 8th, 1917, he went to France and was killed on May 27th, while engaged in an Artillery observation patrol.

His brother officers spoke with the greatest enthusiasm of his charm as a companion, with intense admiration of his courage, and with infinite regret for his loss. And in particular his Colonel wrote:

"I am specially proud of him . . . He has died a credit to his Country and his Corps, and to the 'Greys', and I can give no man a higher testimonial than this."

He was buried in La Chapelette British Cemetery, Peronne.

LIEUT. J. P. THORNE

5th South Staffordshire Regiment

JOHN PARRY THORNE, younger son of George Rennie Thorne, Esquire, M.P. for East Wolverhampton, was born on November 7th, 1888. He was educated at Tettenhall College, Staffordshire, and passed the final examination of the Incorporated Law Society with Honours; on being admitted a solicitor, he practised with his father. He enlisted as a private in September, 1914, and proceeded overseas early in 1915, serving in France, Belgium and Egypt. At the instance of his Commanding Officer he received a commission for gallantry in the field and at his request remained with the regiment, acting first as Signalling and later as Bombing Officer. He was killed near Gommecourt on July 1st, 1916, while leading a bombing party into a German trench from which he never returned.

His name is perpetuated on the Thiepval Memorial.

PRIVATE W. E. THORNE

10th Essex Regiment

WILLIAM EWARTT THORNE, son of Will James Thorne, Esquire, M.P. for the Plaistow Division of West Ham since 1906, was born on July 6th, 1886. He was educated at Credon Road School, Plaistow, and at the outbreak of War was in the employment of the Corporation of West Ham as a carpenter and joiner. He enlisted in the Essex Regiment on November 2nd, 1914, and went overseas on December 29th, 1916. He was reported wounded and missing at Ypres on August 12th, 1917, and reported killed on August 8th, 1918. It would appear that he was wounded and carried to a dressing station, which was afterwards bombed and everyone in it blown up.

His name is perpetuated on the Menin Gate Memorial, Ypres.

LIEUT. E. S. TURTON

Yorkshire Hussars

EDMUND SPENCER TURTON, only child of Sir Edmund R. Turton, Bart., M.P for the Thirsk and Malton Division (Yorks. N.R.), 1915-29, was born on May 14th, 1889. He was educated at Eton, where he was Captain of the Oppidans and also of his House.

Frank, cheerful, good-humoured, he had marked social gifts, while there was a deep seriousness in his character which was appreciated by those who knew him best. While still at Eton he was elected to I Zingari, a club of which his grandfather was the founder, and was naturally the youngest member of it. In 1908 he went up to Balliol College, Oxford, took honours in Classical Moderations and in Law and was called to the Bar in 1913, with every prospect of becoming prominent in public life. Before leaving Oxford he had received a commission in the Yorkshire Hussars (he was a fearless rider in point-to-point races and was well known in the hunting-field), and in February he went to the front with his squadron. The War Office had just arranged for him to return to England with the temporary rank of Captain, to assist Lord Feversham in raising the Farmers' Infantry Battalion in Yorkshire. The transfer was, at his own request, delayed for a week so that he might obtain experience of active trench warfare. He was temporarily attached to a battalion of the Sherwood Foresters, and was shot by a sniper outside Ypres on August 30th, 1915.

He was buried in Lijssenthoek Military Cemetery, Poperinghe.

PRIVATE B. WADSWORTH

1/4th York and Lancaster Regiment

BERT WADSWORTH, second son of John Wadsworth, Esquire, M.P. for the Hallam Division of Sheffield, 1906-18, was born on June 22nd, 1881. He was educated locally during the time his father was employed as a coal-miner at the Wharncliffe Silkstone Colliery, Tankersley, near Barnsley. He became Clerk to the Yorkshire Miners' Association and enlisted on March 14th, 1917, proceeding overseas with his regiment the following September. He fell in action at Mount Kemmel on April 29th, 1918, and his name is perpetuated on the Tyne Cot Memorial, Passchendaele.

CAPTAIN A. WALSH, M.C.

4th Battalion South Lancashire Regiment

ARTHUR WALSH, eldest son of the Rt. Hon. Stephen Walsh, M.P. for the Ince Division of Lancashire, 1906-29, Secretary of State for War, Jan.-Nov., 1924, was born on April 1st, 1892. He was educated at Wigan Grammar School, where he won the Powell Scholarship, and at Victoria University, Manchester, graduating M.A. with First Class Honours. He was awarded the Gilchrist Travelling Studentship and a Falkner Fellowship. He was a Licentiate of Letters of the University of Paris and master of Modern Languages and Literature in a Secondary School at Nelson, Lancs. He enlisted at the outbreak of War and went overseas with his regiment in October, 1916. He was wounded near Ypres in September, 1917, fell in action near Givenchy on April 11th, 1918, and his name is perpetuated on the Loos Memorial.

Captain Walsh was awarded the Military Cross.

LIEUT. C. J. WARNER

2nd Battalion Oxfordshire Light Infantry

CORNWALLIS JOHN WARNER, second son of Colonel Sir Courtenay Warner, Bart., C.B., M.P. for the Lichfield Division of Staffordshire, 1896-1923, was born on February 1st, 1889. He was educated at Eton and Christ Church, Oxford, and was called to the Bar in 1911. He obtained a commission in the Oxfordshire Light Infantry and proceeded overseas in December, 1914. He was reported missing, believed killed, at Festubert, on May 16th, 1915, and his name is perpetuated on the Memorial at Le Touret.

SECOND LIEUT. T. H. B. WEBB

Welsh Guards

THOMAS HARRY BASIL WEBB, only son of Lieut.-Colonel Sir Henry Webb, Bart., M.P. for the Forest of Dean Division of Gloucestershire, 1911-18, was born on August 12th, 1898. He was educated at Sandroyd School and Winchester, where he excelled both at cricket and football. He was gazetted to the Welsh Guards shortly after leaving Winchester, just before his nineteenth birthday, and proceeded overseas with his regiment. He fell in action on November 30th, 1917, while leading his men to the assault of a German position at Gouzeaucourt. The whole Guards Division were engaged in this counter-attack, and it fell to the 1st Battalion Welsh Guards and the 4th Battalion Grenadier Guards to attack the south end of the village; they were met by a burst of machine-gun fire, and Lieut. Webb fell that moment killed. He was buried in Gouzeaucourt New British Cemetery.

PRIVATE J. N. WILLIAMS

Auckland Battalion, New Zealand Expeditionary Force

JOHN NATHANIEL WILLIAMS, elder son of Colonel Sir Robert Williams, Bart., M.P. for West Dorset 1895-1922, was born on January 24th, 1878. He was educated at Eton and New College, Oxford. He enlisted in New Zealand in August, 1914, and landed in Egypt with the New Zealand Expeditionary Force the following November. He fell in the first attack on Gallipoli on April 25th, 1915, and his name is perpetuated on the Lone Pine Memorial, Gallipoli.

LIEUT. W. YOUNG

2nd Cameron Highlanders

WILLIAM YOUNG, elder son of William Young, Esquire, M.P. for East Perth, 1910, and for the Perth Division of Perth and Kinross, 1918-22, was born on January 3rd, 1893. He was educated at the Grammar School and Gordon's College, Aberdeen, and at Leys School, Cambridge. He played football for the Old Leysians and the London Scottish Football Clubs. He had been employed in a merchant's office in the City for some months when War was declared and joined the 1st Battalion London Scottish on September 14th, 1914. He served with them all through the first winter of the War, obtaining a commission in May, 1915, and was then posted to the 2nd Cameron Highlanders. He was severely wounded near Salonica in 1916, and was subsequently killed in action near Ypres on August 22nd, 1917, whilst leading his men and cheering them forward. His name is perpetuated on the Tyne Cot Memorial, Passchendaele.

LIEUT. C. F. YOUNGER

The Lothians and Border Horse

CHARLES FREARSON YOUNGER, youngest son of Sir George Younger, Bart., M.P. for Ayr Burghs from 1906 until his elevation to the Peerage in 1923 as 1st Viscount Younger, was born on September 9th, 1885. He was educated at Winchester and New College, Oxford. He was Head of his House at Winchester and in Sixth Book his last year (1904) and played at Lord's in 1903 and 1904; he was also a good racquets player, being third string to the late Captain E. L. Wright and the Hon. C. N. Bruce in 1904 when they won the Public Schools Championship. Lieut. Younger was a director of George Younger & Son, brewers, Alloa, Scotland, and joined up on the first day of mobilization.

He fell mortally wounded at St. Léger, near Albert, on March 20th, 1917, died the next day at Aveluy, and was buried in Aveluy Communal Cemetery.

V.

SONS OF OFFICERS
OF THE
HOUSE OF COMMONS

LIEUT. A. R. GARTON

6th Northumberland Fusiliers

ARTHUR RICHMOND GARTON, eldest son of Lieut.-Col. W. G. A. Garton, O.B.E., of the Admission Order Office, House of Commons, was born on December 10th, 1880. He was educated privately and was employed as a Clerk in the Bank of England. He was a lieutenant in the Civil Service Rifles and transferred to the 6th Battalion Northumberland Fusiliers, proceeding overseas with them on April 20th, 1915. He fell in his first engagement near Ypres on April 26th, 1915, and his name is perpetuated on the Menin Gate Memorial, Ypres.

Lieut. Garton was mentioned in despatches.

LIEUT. R. W. GARTON

11th South Lancashire Regiment

REGINALD WILLIAM GARTON, youngest son of Lieut.-Col. W. G. A. Garton, O.B.E., of the Admission Order Office, House of Commons, was born on March 8th, 1897. He was educated at Christ's Hospital, West Horsham, Sussex, and joined the Civil Service Rifles on the outbreak of War. He transferred later to the 11th Battalion South Lancashire Regiment and served in France with it from October 31st, 1915, until he fell in action at the Battle of the Somme on July 1st, 1916.

His name is perpetuated on the Thiepval Memorial.

SECOND LIEUT. E. W. J. JOHNSON

7th Bedfordshire Regiment

EVELYN WALTER JAMES JOHNSON, only son of Mr. A. C. Johnson, second doorkeeper at the House of Commons, was born on April 9th, 1897. He was educated at Emanuel School, Wandsworth, and was employed as a Clerk in Lloyds Bank. He was gazetted Second Lieutenant on January 21st, 1915, and went overseas on March 24th, 1916. He was wounded before Mametz by shell fire on June 26th and died of his wounds in No. 2 Red Cross Hospital at Rouen on July 20th, 1916. He was buried in St. Sever Cemetery, Rouen.

SECOND LIEUT. B. MOON

Post Office Rifles

BASIL MOON, second son of Sir Ernest Moon, K.C.B., K.C., Counsel to the Speaker of the House of Commons, 1907-28, was born on August 31st, 1884. He was educated at Eton and Magdalen College, Oxford, where he was one of those men who without being specially distinguished in games or work are just the most valuable part of a College for the steady influence on the right side that they exert. On leaving Oxford he spent some months at Angers learning French, and, in 1909, became qualified as a Chartered Accountant. He then lived for a time in Germany, and spent the following years mainly in Russia, having embarked on a business career.

When War was declared, he at once applied for a commission and was appointed second lieutenant in the Post Office Rifles. He was mortally wounded at Festubert on the morning of May 24th, 1915, while most gallantly leading his Platoon directly behind the bombing party in an attack up a long trench half held by the Post Office Rifles and half by the Germans. His fine example, coolness, and courage helped materially towards the success of the attack on that occasion, and it was without doubt largely owing to his behaviour that the slight check experienced at the beginning of the attack was overcome. He died of his wounds the following day and was buried in the Post Office Rifles Cemetery, Festubert.

The great principle of his life was perseverance. Whatever he did, he devoted his whole mind to; and his industry was remarkable in the mastery of the details of anything that he took in hand. With a great charm of manner and a delightful humour, he was widely loved as a friend and companion, and by all classes of people among whom he lived.

Lieut. Moon was mentioned in despatches.

LIEUT. W. D. NICHOLSON

2nd Cameron Highlanders

WILLIAM DUKINFIELD NICHOLSON, second son of Sir Arthur W. Nicholson, K.C.B., Clerk Assistant, House of Commons, was born on May 13th, 1888. He was educated at Marlborough College and Magdalen College, Oxford. He was in the Trial Eights when Magdalen was Head of the River and winner of the Grand Challenge Cup at Henley in 1910. He was gazetted to the Queen's Own Cameron Highlanders and joined them at Bangalore, India, in 1910. While in India he gained considerable distinction in athletics. He accompanied his battalion to France in December, 1914, and fell in action at St. Eloi, on February 23rd, 1915, while trying to bring in a wounded comrade. He was buried in Dickebusch New Military Cemetery.

LIEUT. A. S. NICHOLSON

1st Cameron Highlanders

ARTHUR STUART NICHOLSON, third son of Sir Arthur W. Nicholson, K.C.B., Clerk Assistant, House of Commons, was born on September 18th, 1889. He was educated at Winchester College and obtained his commission in the 1st Battalion Cameron Highlanders in 1909. In 1913 he was appointed A.D.C. to Lord Glenconner, when High Commissioner to the General Assembly of the Church of Scotland, and in 1914 to General Sir J. Spenser Ewart, K.C.B., General Officer Commanding-in-Chief, Scottish Command.

When War broke out he rejoined his battalion and served with the 1st Division through the Retreat from Mons and the Battle of the Marne.

He fell at the Battle of the Aisne on September 14th, 1914, and his name is perpetuated on the Memorial at La Ferté.

SECOND LIEUT. G. NORMAN

11th Royal Fusiliers

GARNET NORMAN, only son of Mr. George Norman, Messenger, House of Commons, was born on March 25th, 1895. He was educated at Christ's Hospital and was employed as a clerk in the London and South-Western Bank. He enlisted on August 27th, 1914, in the 6th Battalion Duke of Cornwall's Light Infantry. He was recommended for and obtained a commission, proceeding overseas in December, 1916. He fell in action at Hangard on April 2nd, 1918, and his name is perpetuated on the Pozières Memorial.

SERGEANT P. J. TURTLE

13th London Regiment

PERCY JOHN TURTLE, only son of Mr. Richard Turtle, Messenger (First Class) in the Department of the Serjeant-At-Arms, House of Commons, was born on March 19th, 1897. He was educated at Sir Walter St. John's School, Battersea, and was subsequently employed as a Boy Clerk in the Registry of Friendly Societies' Office in Westminster. He enlisted in September, 1914, and was promoted Corporal in 1915. He served in Ireland, France and Palestine. Having won his marksman's badge, he was made Musketry Instructor in Home Camps. He was wounded at Vimy Ridge in August, 1916, and promoted Sergeant for gallantry. The following year he was serving in Egypt and Palestine, and fell in action at Beersheba on October 31st, 1917. He was buried in Beersheba War Cemetery.

VI.

APPENDIX

The annexed lists show the position of the graves of all those whose names are on the Parliamentary War Memorial, Westminster Hall, except Members and Officers of the House of Lords.

The following abbreviations have been used:—

    Cem. = Cemetery
    Mil. Cem. = Military Cemetery
    Com. Cem. = Communal Cemetery
    Chyd. = Churchyard
    Ext. = Extension
    Brit. = British

Where the entry reads "Menin Gate Memorial," "Arras Memorial," etc., it means that the body was not recovered and the name is recorded on the memorial mentioned.

The "missing" of the Royal Navy, i.e. those who were lost at Sea and whose bodies were never found, have been commemorated on memorials at the three home ports.

I. MEMBERS OF THE HOUSE OF COMMONS

Capt. the Hon. T. C. R. Agar-Robartes	Coldstream Guards	Lapugnoy Mil. Cem., Plot I, Row D, Grave 33
Lt.-Col. the Hon. G. V. Baring	Coldstream Guards	Citadel New Mil. Cem., Fricourt, Plot II, Row A, Grave 9
Major F. Bennett-Goldney	Special List and Staff	St. Germain-en-Laye Old Com. Cem., Division K, Grave 79
Lt.-Col. D. F. Campbell, D.S.O.	Black Watch	Kilmarnock Cem., Ayrshire, Compt. L (New portion) Grave 28
Capt. H. T. Cawley	Manchester Regt.	Lancashire Landing Cem., Helles, Gallipoli, Row A, Grave 76
Capt. the Hon. O. Cawley	Shropshire Yeo.	Néry Com. Cem.
Lt.-Col. P. A. Clive, D.S.O.	Gren. Guards att. Lancs. Fus.	Arras Memorial
Lt.-Col. Lord N. E. Crichton-Stuart	Welch Regt.	Béthune Town Cem., Plot III, Row M, Grave 10
Capt. J. J. Esmonde	R.A.M.C.	Terryglass R.C. Chyd., Co. Tipperary

Major V. Fleming, D.S.O.	Q.O. Oxfordshire Hussars	Ste Emilie Brit. Cem. Villers-Faucon, Plot II, Row D, Grave 3
Lieut. W. G. C. Gladstone	R. Welch Fus.	Hawarden (St. Deiniol) Chyd., Flintshire
Major P. K. Glazebrook, D.S.O.	Cheshire Yeo.	Jerusalem War Cem., Plot O, Grave 106
Lieut. T. M. Kettle	R. Dublin Fus.	Thiepval Memorial
Major the Hon. C. H. Lyell	R.G.A.	Arlington National Cem., Fort Myer, Virginia, U.S.A., Lot 4140, Southern Division, Officers' Section (East side of lot)
Lieut. the Hon. F. W. S. McLaren	R.F.C.	Busbridge (St. John the Baptist) Chyd., Surrey
Lieut. the Hon. C. T. Mills	Scots Guards	Loos Memorial, Panel 8, Column 1
Capt. the Hon. A. E. B. O'Neill	Life Guards	Menin Gate Memorial, Ypres, Panel 3, Column 1
Capt. the Hon. N. J. A. Primrose, M.C.	R. Bucks Hussars	Ramleh War Cem., Palestine, Plot D, Grave 49
Lieut. Viscount Quenington	R. Gloucestershire Hussars	Cairo New British Protestant Cem., Plot G
Major W. H. K. Redmond	R. Irish Regt.	Isolated grave in garden of Locre Hospice
Lt. Col. Lord A. G. Thynne, D.S.O.	Wilts Regt.	Béthune Town Cem., Plot II, Row L, Grave 13
Lieut. the Hon. W. L. C. Walrond	R.A.S.C.	Bradfield (All Saints) Chyd., Uffculme, Devon

II. OFFICERS OF THE HOUSE OF COMMONS

Lieut. R. N. M. Bailey	E. Riding Yeo.	Cairo War Memorial Cem., Plot O, Grave 44
Lieut. R. W. T. Cox	Dorset Regt.	Spoilbank Cem., Zillebeke, Plot I, Row K, Grave 9
Lieut. V. W. D. Fox	Irish Guards	Le Touret Mil. Cem., Richebourg-l'Avoué, Plot II, Row A, Grave 19
Major H. S. Green	London Regt.	Tyne Cot Cem., Passchendaele, Plot VIII, Row C, Grave 5
Corpl. R. Lanchbery	R. Highlanders	La Neuville Brit. Cem., Corbie, Plot I, Row C, Grave 34
Lieut. W. K. Sanderson	Border Regt.	Thiepval Memorial
Lieut. F. Seymour	K.R.R.C.	Menin Gate Memorial, Ypres, Panel 51, Column 4

III. SONS OF MEMBERS OF THE HOUSE OF COMMONS

L/Corpl. J. C. Adamson	Seaforth Highlanders	Thiepval Memorial
Lieut. J. S. Ainsworth	Hussars	Méteren Mil. Cem., Plot IV, Row E, Grave 677
Lt.-Col. D. K. Anderson, M.C.	W. Kent Regt.	Cambrai Memorial, Panel 3, Column 3
Lieut. C. K. Anderson	R. West Kent Regt.	Hautrage Mil. Cem., Plot I, Row D, Grave 17
Capt. the Hon. A. Annesley	Hussars	Ypres Town Cem. (Menin Gate), Plot I, Row E 1, Grave 19
Lieut. D. M. Archdale	King's African Rifles	Iringa Cem., E. Africa, Plot V, Row A, Grave 13
Lieut. R. Asquith	Grenadier Guards	Guillemont Road Cem., Guillemont, Plot I, Row B, Grave 3
2/Lieut. A. S. Balfour	R.F.A. & R.F.C.	Tincourt New Brit. Cem., Plot IV, Row E, Grave 18
Capt. C. W. Banbury	Coldstream Guards	Soupir Com. Cem., Row A, Grave 2
2/Lieut. H. Barnes	Gordon Highlanders	Dud Corner Cem., Loos, Plot IX, Row E, Grave 2

Capt. N. Barran	Life Guards	Windsor (Spital) Cem., Berks.
2/Lieut. E. A. Beauchamp	Coldstream Guards	Lillers Com. Cem., Plot I, Row B, Grave 4
2/Lieut. F. H. Bethell	Connaught Rangers	Menin Gate Memorial, Ypres, Panel 42, Column 3
2/Lieut. H. F. Boles	Lancers & R.F.C.	Bailleul Com. Cem. Ext., Plot I, Row F, Grave 34
Lieut. H. J. Boyton	Grenadier Guards	Combles Com. Cem. Ext., Plot II, Row C, Grave 12
Paymaster Sub-Lieut. W. P. Brace	R.N.V.R.	Newport (St. Woolos) Cem., Monmouthshire
2/Lieut. G. C. Brassey	Coldstream Guards	Mory Street Mil. Cem., St. Léger, Row A, Grave 4
2/Lieut. A. H. R. Burn	R. Dragoons	Menin Gate Memorial, Ypres, Panel 5, Column 1
Lt.-Com. P. S. Campbell	R.N.V.R.	Ancre Brit. Cem., Beaumont-Hamel, Plot II, Row D, Grave 44
2/Lieut. F. L. Carew	Hussars	Menin Gate Memorial, Ypres, Panel 5, Column 7
Major E. H. H. Carlile	Herts Yeo.	Arras Memorial
2/Lieut. D. A. Carnegie	R.F.A.	Ferme-Oliver Brit. Cem., Elverdinghe, Plot III, Row C, Grave 2
Major J. S. Cawley	Hussars	Néry Com. Cem.

Capt. R. G. H. Chaloner	Wilts Regt.	Calais Southern Cem., Officers' Plot, Row A, Grave 15
2/Lieut. A. J. F. Chambers	Warwickshire Yeo.	Kantara War Memorial Cem., Egypt, Plot D, Grave 10
Lt. Col. T. V. B. Denniss	R. Berks Regt.	Hillingdon Cem., Middlesex
2/Lieut. G. J. Esmonde	Northumberland Fus.	Cité Bonjean Mil. Cem., Armentières, Plot III, Row A, Grave 18
Midshipman J. H. G. Esmonde	Royal Navy	Portsmouth Memorial, Panel 11
Capt. J. E. Fiennes	Gordon Highlanders	Duisans Brit. Cem., Plot III, Row L, Grave 16
The Rev. J. Fitzgibbon, M.C.	Chaplain to the Forces	Trefcon Brit. Cem., Caulaincourt, Row B, Grave 56
Lieut. M. J. Fitzgibbon	R. Dublin Fus.	Helles Memorial, Gallipoli, Panel 191, Column 1
Capt. M. A. Fitzroy	Seaforth Highlanders	Cabaret-Rouge Brit. Cem., Souchez, Plot XVII, Row C, Grave 22
2/Lieut. J. Forster	K.R.R.C.	La Ferté Memorial, Panel 23, Column 1
Lieut. A. H. Forster	Dragoons	Exbury (St. Catherine) Church, Hampshire. (Body was cremated, and ashes deposited under the Altar in Church.)

Capt. W. Harmood-Banner	South Wales Borderers	Cambrin Chyd. Ext., Plot I, Row A, Grave 12
Capt. D. Henderson	Middlesex Regt.	London Cem., High Wood, Longueval, Row A, Grave 13
Lieut. C. C. Henry	Worcester Regt.	Loos Memorial, Panel 64, Column 1
Capt. G. G. Hermon-Hodge	R.H.A.	Gézaincourt Com. Cem. Ext., Plot I, Row B, Grave 12
2/Lieut. J. P. Hermon-Hodge	Oxford & Bucks Light Inf.	Rifle House Mil. Cem., Warneton, Plot III, Row F, Grave 1
2/Lieut. G. M. Hewart	Lincoln Regt.	Green Hill Cem., Suvla, Gallipoli, Plot II, Row B, Grave 1
Capt. C. G. R. Hibbert	L.N. Lancs. Regt.	Le Touret Memorial, Panel 27, Column 3
Lieut. W. P. Hinds	R. Welch Fus.	Merville Com. Cem., Plot VII, Row A, Grave 5
2/Lieut. I. G. John	South Wales Borderers	St. Mary's A.D.S. Cem., Haisnes, Special Memorial
Capt. J. K. Law	R. Fus. & R.F.C.	Arras Memorial
Lieut. C. J. Law	K.O. Scottish Borderers	Gaza War Cem., Palestine, Plot VII, Row A, Grave 9
Lieut. H. Logan	Leicester Yeo.	Tournai Com. Cem. Allied Ext., Plot IV, Row G, Grave 10
Brig.-Gen. W. Long, C.M.G., D.S.O.	R. Scots Greys	Couin Brit. Cem., Plot VI, Row C, Grave 19

Lieut. G. A. Loyd	Scots Guards	Poperinghe Com. Cem., Plot I, Row B, Grave 4
Lieut. D. C. D. MacMaster	Cameron Highlanders	Dud Corner Cem., Loos, Plot IV, Row C, Grave 12
2/Lieut. G. T. G. McMicking	Cambridge Regt.	Orthen Protestant Cem., Holland
Capt. G. C. N. Nicholson	R.F.C.	Hurley (St. Mary the Virgin) Chyd., Berkshire
Lieut. W. H. E. Nield	R. Fus.	Dantzig Alley Brit. Cem., Mametz, Plot III, Row O, Grave 8
2/Lieut. H. N. Nuttall	R.A.S.C.	Lijssenthoek Mil. Cem., Poperinghe, Plot XIII, Row A, Grave 4
2/Lieut. W. J. O'Malley	R.F.A.	Bedford House Cemetery, Zillebeke, Enclosure No. 4, Plot I, Row H, Grave 13
Lieut. W. P. Orde-Powlett	Yorks Regt.	Menin Gate Memorial, Ypres, Panel 33, Column 9
2/Lieut. G. V. Pearce	R. Warwick Regt.	Ploegsteert Memorial, Panel 2, Column 7
Lieut. R. H. P. Pease	Coldstream Guards	Guards Cem., Lesboeufs, Plot XIII, Row P, Grave 2
Lieut. T. W. Pollard	Lancashire Fus.	Arras Memorial
Capt. C. T. A. Pollock	E. Yorks Regt. & O.T.C.	Moreuil Com. Cem. Allied Ext., Row C, Grave 1

Lieut. R. J. Prothero	Hussars	Baghdad War Cemetery, Plot IX, Row C, Grave 6
Sub-Lieut. J. F. Royds	Royal Navy	Fulbeck (St. Nicholas) Chyd., Lincs, Nth. pte. enclosure, Row 3, Grave 1
2/Lieut. T. W. Russell	R. Dublin Fus.	Knightsbridge Cem., Mesnil-Martinsart, Row C, Grave 1
2/Lieut. J. H. Salter	King's Own Royal Lancs. Regt.	Loos Memorial, Panel 19, Column 1
Capt. A. P. I. Samuels	R. Irish Rifles	Ration Farm (La Plus Douve) Annexe, Ploegsteert, Plot II, Row B, Grave 25
Capt. C. G. Seely	Hampshire Regt.	Gaza War Cem., Palestine, Plot XXI, Row E, Grave 12
2/Lieut. F. R. Seely	Hampshire Regt.	Haute-Avesnes Brit. Cem., Plot I, Row C, Grave 14
2/Lieut. D. J. Sheehan	R.F.C.	Cabaret-Rouge Brit. Cem., Souchez, Plot XVI, Row N, Grave 16
2/Lieut. M. J. Sheehan	R.A.F.	Anneux Brit. Cem., Plot I, Row H, Grave 21
Lieut. W. E. D. Shortt	Scots Guards	Bleuet Farm Brit. Cem., Elverdinghe, Plot I, Row A, Grave 22
Lieut. J. F. Smallwood, M.C.	Middlesex Regt.	Etaples Mil. Cem., Plot XVII, Row D, Grave 20

Capt. E. B. Smallwood, M.C.	Hertford Regt.	Essex Farm Cem., Boesinghe, Plot II, Row S, Grave 22
Major G. H. Soames	West Yorks Regt.	Cambrin Chyd. Ext., Plot I, Row T, Grave 18
Major M. G. Soames	R.F.A.	Heilly Station Cem., Méricourt-l'Abbé, Plot IV, Row G, Grave 30
Lieut. C. Stanton	Welch Regt.	No Man's Cot Brit. Cem., Boesinghe, Row B, Grave 1
Lieut. V. A. Strauss	R.A.S.C. & R.F.C.	Arras Memorial
2/Lieut. H. Tennant	Scots Greys & R.F.C.	La Chapelette Brit. Cem., Peronne, Plot I, Row B, Grave 7
Lieut. J. P. Thorne	S. Staffs Regt.	Thiepval Memorial
Pte. W. Thorne	Essex Regt.	Menin Gate Memorial, Ypres, Panel 39, Column 5
Lieut. E. S. Turton	Yorkshire Hussars	Lijssenthoek Mil. Cem., Poperinghe, Plot I, Row A, Grave 16
Pte. B. Wadsworth	York & Lancs. Regt.	Tyne Cot Memorial, Passchendaele, Panel 128, Column 1
Capt. A. Walsh, M.C.	South Lancs. Regt.	Loos Memorial, Panel 76, Column 1
Lieut. C. J. Warner	Oxford & Bucks Light Inf.	Le Touret Memorial, Panel 26, Column 1

2/Lieut. T. H. B. Webb	Welsh Guards	Gouzeaucourt New Brit. Cem., Plot VI, Row G, Grave 19
Pte. J. N. Williams	New Zealand Exp. Force	Lone Pine Memorial, Gallipoli, Panel 73, Column 1
Lieut. W. Young	Cameron Highlanders	Tyne Cot Memorial, Passchendaele, Panel 136, Column 1
Lieut. C. F. Younger	Lothians & Border Horse	Aveluy Com. Cem. Ext., Row M, Grave 8

IV. SONS OF OFFICERS OF THE HOUSE OF COMMONS

Lieut. A. R. Garton	Northumberland Fus.	Menin Gate Memorial, Ypres, Panel 12, Column 7
Lieut. R. W. Garton	South Lancs. Regt.	Thiepval Memorial
2/Lieut. E. W. J. Johnson	Bedford Regt.	St. Sever Cem., Rouen, Officers' Plot A, Row 4, Grave 4
2/Lieut. B. O. Moon	Post Office Rifles	Post Office Rifles Cem., Festubert, Plot I, Row B, Grave 9
Lieut. W. D. Nicholson	Cameron Highlanders	Dickebusch New Mil. Cem., Plot I, Row A, Grave 19
Lieut. A. S. Nicholson	Cameron Highlanders	La Ferté Memorial, Panel 26, Column 1
2/Lieut. G. Norman	Royal Fusiliers	Pozières Memorial, Panel 19, Column 1
L/Sergt. P. J. Turtle	London Regt.	Beersheba War Cem., Plot N, Grave 54